MY FATHER NEVER
TOOK ME TO A
Baseball Game

My Father Never Took Me To A Baseball Game

Stephen Costello

ISBN: 0692231595
ISBN-13: 978-0692231593

Guillermo

Dreams come
true
this was
mine

Thanks for
reading Omy
still
☺

🙂

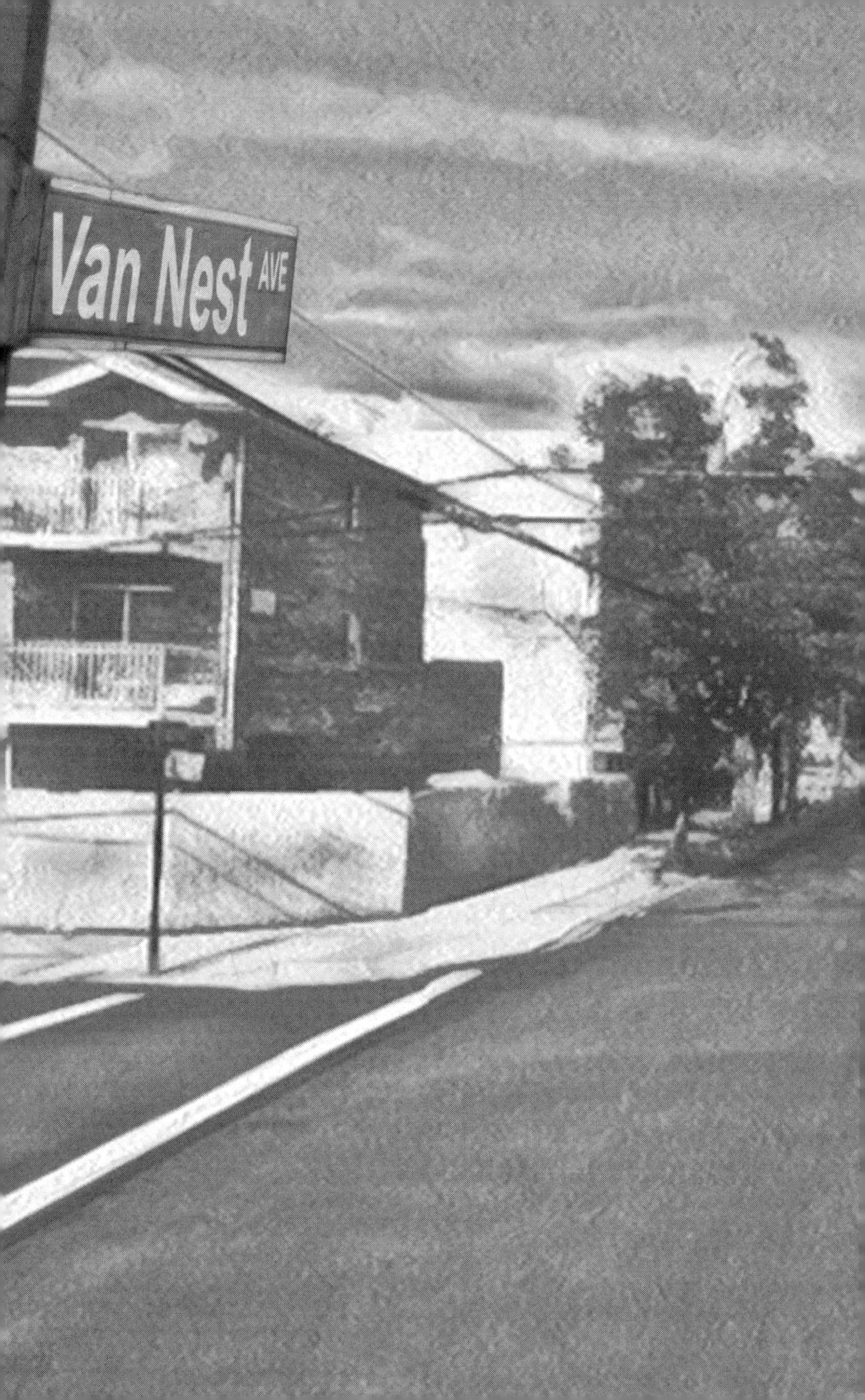
Van Nest AVE

FOREWORD
BY JEFFREY GITOMER

In 1954, at age 8, my father took me to watch my first professional baseball game. The Philadelphia Athletics played the Boston Red Sox. I watched Ted Williams hit a home run, and became a baseball fan, then a sports fan, for life. I remember that day, just like every kid remembers the day at his dad took him or her to the "first game." Handed down from father to child, it's a rite of passage. But more than that, it's a memory. A lifetime memory. Events become both memories and lessons that last a lifetime.

Stephen Costello and I became instant friends. I was introduced to him through my relationship and friendship with Brandon Steiner. In spite of being a New Yorker, Costello is warm, friendly, engaging, giving, and has an overwhelmingly strong sense of family. I am the same. Whoever said, "opposites attract" was referring to magnets not people.

Our friendship began exchanging sports stories. Games attended. Memories of events. People we know or knew. We learned from each other and we laughed out loud. And without revealing too much of the contents of the book, we both shared a deep admiration for the quasi-perfect game thrown by Harvey Haddix in 1959.

For a lot of reasons, I knew a lot about the game. So did Costello, and we talked about it all the time. Of course I had to tell him about the day my dad took me to my first baseball game to see Ted Williams play. Expecting him to counter with his "first game with dad" story, he responded, "My father never took me to a ball game." I was stunned.

As our friendship grew stronger, we began to exchange family stories, and family lessons. Parents, children, spouses, and assorted events that have shaped our philosophies and lives. Emotional exchanges that cemented our relationship. Especially those of family. We learn to parent from our parents and our friends parents…both what to do, and what not to do. Then we become parents…and the legacy continues to our kids.

When Steve said, "I'm writing a book," and told me some of the contents, both family and sports, I immediately volunteered to write the foreword. I wanted to write it so that I could reinforce the emotions and the feelings that he has shared with me throughout our friendship.

Stephen Costello's joys and sorrows will corroborate many of yours. His messages transferred here, will make you laugh, cry, and think. Stories about family, stories about success, stories about failure, stories about life, and of course stories about baseball.

If you're old like me, you recall there was much less political sensitivity in the 1960's. Injustice was settled with a fight after school, not in a courtroom or in the media. This book is a remembrance and a memoir of those days and those times. And how they relate to these days and these times. And you're going to love it.

Here's how to read this book: once for enjoyment, and once for learning. Each of us reads to gain insight. Whether you want to admit it or not, often the things you read about relate to your life, even though someone else is writing about their life. This is such a book. Just reading the title of this book, "My Father Never Took Me to a Baseball Game," immediately makes you think of your father taking you to your first ballgame. It did for me. Vividly. And the fact that his father never did, compels you to find out "why."

If you're a fan of family, you're going to be a fan of this book. If you're a fan of compelling stories, you're going to be a fan of this book. If you're a fan of life, you're going to be a fan of this book. And, if you're a fan of baseball, you're going to be a fan of this book. Whether you're in an armchair, on the subway, in an airplane seat, or on the beach, this book will create enjoyment, and Stephen's memories and lessons will revive many of yours – and isn't that what life is all about?

-Jeffrey Gitomer

Friend, Father, and Grandfather

Jeffrey Gitomer is the author of many New York Times Best Sellers and Amazon.com Number One Best Sellers including *The Little Red Book of Selling, The Little Gold Book of YES! Attitude*, and *The Little Book of Leadership*.

CONTENTS

MY FATHER NEVER TOOK ME
TO A BASEBALL GAME

Inchworms were always a huge problem growing up. Our entire property would be inundated with thousands of tiny green inchworms hanging from the oak trees in our back yard. Inchworm removal came from the same guys every year; a six foot tall fat guy in a dirty white T-shirt and a little muscle guy with 'We Spray Inchworms' on his tattered company shirt. Every spring they would drive slowly down Hetty's Path (our block). You would stop them the same way as you would the ice cream man.

So as with all our household vendors, my father would negotiate the price in the driveway, with the little muscle man and the fat guy. He's now calling the little guy "Short Stack" and the fat guy "Fatso." My father made up offensive nickname for everybody. They tell my father that this year it's seventy bucks to spray the inchworms. After an awkward pause, he runs into the house, and I casually follow him. I see him pull out the bread basket from the drawer in the kitchen counter that doubles as his personal filing cabinet for all the bills. He searches in a panic, and then he yells out to me. "I found it!"

He runs past me, out the door, back into the driveway and shouts, "I only paid 60 bucks last year! I'll give you fifty this year and you'll be happy about it!" They didn't really look that happy about it. The next thing that happened ranks as a top childhood memory of mine: Fatso says, "Fuck you, it's seventy or we get back in the truck." It seemed they were not at all afraid of my father, and I loved it.

Feeling emasculated in front of his son, he screamed that they could kiss his ass as they didn't use anything but water in the inch worm spraying machine. They were ripping him off every year, he ranted. Just from the odor of the guys and their truck, it certainly smelled to me like some form of pesticides were involved. It didn't seem like just water. Also, I remembered sweeping up thousands of dead inchworms last year the day after they sprayed. The ones that survived weren't heading to a butterfly exhibit anytime soon. Fatso said, "If you think it's only water then I guess you won't mind drinking some." He pointed the spray hose in my father's face. Fatso and Short Stack both started laughing. My father goes into another rage. He leaps at Fatso and punches him right in the face. Fatso stands in shock for a moment, bleeding. He then puts my father in a headlock, while Short Stack jumps into the action and starts punching, kicking, and biting him until they have him on the ground. This is getting serious. I'm seeing blood everywhere and my heart is racing. I know it's time to go get some help, so I run into the house yelling, "Mommmmm!" Mom is in the kitchen. "Mom the two bug guys are

(*Weaponry to fight the "Bug Guys"*)

outside beating up dad." She runs back outside with me. As we get outside, we see the guys take off, leaving my father there on the ground. Dazed, he slowly gets up, walks over to his truck, a 1973 Green Blazer, and reaches inside. It appears that he's gathering weapons. He yells at me to jump in the truck. He's holding a blackjack and hands me a tire iron. We're searching for the guys driving about eighty miles an hour down residential streets. We're in pursuit of revenge. I didn't know what I was doing, but I was glad to be holding a weapon. It was exciting, and that day I learned an incredible lesson.

You can stand up to a bully and win, even if that bully was my father.

After forty minutes of driving, my father passed a gas station. He looked at the sign and noticed that gas was forty cents a gallon. He declared these assholes weren't worth the cost of gas, and called off the search. He didn't get the revenge he hoped for. I saw him lift a piece of napkin from the console of the Blazer. He wiped away some blood dripping by his eye. As I looked over at him he looked away. The bully knew I saw someone get the better of him. This day somehow never made it to his war chest of stories, and we had plenty of living inchworms that year for me to sweep up. The story was hidden deeply in the family secrets. A mention of it would have me on the ground bleeding.

Yeah, my father never took me to a baseball game and my hero is a great baseball player that you probably have never heard of. He was little, he was very quiet, and he stood up to bullies his whole life. But let's start the story in 1959, two years before I was born.

ALMOST PERFECT

May 26, 1959 was a special day. That's the day that an unknown farm boy named **Harvey Haddix** (Pittsburg Pirates) threw the greatest game ever pitched in the history of baseball. Yes, in the history of baseball! Harvey Haddix, my hero. Thirty-six men up, and thirty-six men down without a hit, a walk, or an error. Since May 4, 1871, in the 140 years of organized baseball, Harvey Haddix has been the only pitcher ever to go 12 perfect innings. EVER!

The fact that the game was lost by his teammate's error in the 13th inning, with a final score of 2-0 (Milwaukee Braves) is bad luck, an incredible twist of fate, or a combination of the two. Whitey Ford, Sandy Koufax, Tom Seaver, Cy Young, Randy Johnson…I bet you've heard of those guys. Why is Harvey not a household name? How did Harvey get so misplaced in history, and can I get him back in the history books? Why is it that nobody has ever heard of Harvey Haddix? Well, you've probably never heard of me either, but by the end of this book, I hope you will get to know both of us a little bit better. We'll take you on a journey where you will hear both of our stories—his and mine.

Think of how many millions of things had to happen to me from being born in Jacobi Hospital in the Bronx…to 52 years later, becoming the Paul Revere of the greatest game ever pitched. The name Harvey Haddix is far from the banter of baseball conversationalists. The most serious sports fans have never ever heard of Harvey. In a funny way, my writing career has a chance to be similar to Harvey Haddix's baseball career. My writing career has been perfect in fumbling away missed opportunities: not keeping my eye on the ball, or the ball in my glove, or not finishing what I started. Harvey, I know how you feel. Oh, do I ever know how you feel. But I'm finally ready to go the distance in telling both our stories! Right now though, I am intently awakening memories as I furiously make notes with my left hand. Harvey was a lefty, too! Call me a late bloomer to the world of finally being a published writer. Perfection in baseball has been found only 21 times in over one hundred and fifty years. There was a time when baseball went thirty-three years between perfect games, and more people have orbited the earth than there have been perfect games. Next to the 'perfects' are the 'almost perfects'. Cold sweats and nightmares are what you get when you don't get that last out.

Going way back to a hot 4th of July in 1908, there would be no fireworks for Hooks Wiltse of the Giants. His 'almost perfect' happened when he hit George McQuillan of the Phillies with a wild pitch, and that was that. Twenty six perfect outs would be accomplished twelve more times in the next hundred years. Twelve major league pitchers have been suffering from nightmares ever since.

We all know life can be perfect on occasion - the perfect moment, the perfect trip, the perfect gift, the perfect date…the never ending search for perfection. But life will always be a journey of peaks, valleys, triumphs, and bumps in the road, and occasionally a thing here or there is out of your control. Life and baseball are seldom perfect, but can be perfect on occasion.

Baseball is far from a one man show. A perfect game generally requires a teammate or two or three to make an incredible defensive play. Just ask Don Larsen, who threw a perfect game in the World Series – game five, 1956. This accomplishment has only been done once in baseball history. Gil Hodges had what looked to be a sure double in the top of the fifth, but Mickey Mantle, the famous Yankee center fielder tracked it down to save both the day and the perfect game. The headline in newspapers the following day was, "Imperfect Pitcher Throws Perfect Game." After getting shelled earlier in the World Series, Don Larsen didn't think he would get another chance. But Yankee Manager, Casey Stengel, left the ball in Larsen's shoe that day, indicating that Larsen was pitching against the Brooklyn Dodgers.

So you can lose a perfect game when a teammate screws up, or win a perfect game when a teammate makes an amazing play. Such was the case with Harvey. As a pitcher you need a little bit of luck, some good fielding, and an incredible defensive play or two. You can have 27 up, 27 down and forever be known as baseball royalty. If you are ever short a little cash, you can sign a baseball with the date of the perfect game, and sell it for up to $500.

After Harvey Haddix's famous game, Lew Burdette (Milwaukee Braves) told the media, "I called Harvey that night in the visiting clubhouse. I told him I realize I got what I wanted, a win, but I'd really give it up because you pitched the greatest game that's ever been pitched in the history of baseball. It was a damned shame you had to lose." Lew Burdette was the opposing pitcher that refused several times to come out of the game because Harvey was still in the game. There was no way Harvey was coming out of the game, because he was throwing the greatest game in baseball history. I was a devout baseball fan and a little league phenom (so they said) who eventually went on to pitch in college. It is unimaginable how a no-hitter must feel in the big leagues with thousands of fans in the stadium, broadcast on national television. This game was televised to no one…but that's a story for later in this book. Just like in life, someone can outshine all the others, yet still go unnoticed. Allow me to officially introduce you to my hero, Harvey Haddix.

THE REAL HARVEY HADDIX

Harvey was raised on his family's farm that was about 30 miles away from Medway, Ohio. Growing up, the closest Harvey ever got to play real baseball was an occasional pick-up game in the fields surrounding the farm. Often he would see how far he could throw an old, dog-chewed rubber ball. Harvey was a little guy at 5'9 and 150 pounds, but he had strong forearms and wrists from bailing hay and other farm work. Farming was all hard work and long days. The other kids Harvey played ball with were amazed that he threw harder than everyone else, even though he was smaller.

As Hank Aaron would tell me when I interviewed him in 2012, "In baseball, power comes from strong wrists, and strong forearms." Hank would not fare well against Harvey in that 1959 game, as all he could muster was an intentional walk in the thirteenth inning. Even Hank Aaron, the greatest home run hitter of all time, didn't have one hit that day.

Harvey, a diehard Red Legs fan, (the Cincinnati Reds went by this name for part of the 1950's to avoid any perceived association with communism), would fall asleep at night listening to their games on the radio, dreaming of running the bases atop his very own field of dreams. It wouldn't be until his senior year at Westville High School that Harvey played his first organized ball game. Harvey had a bit of good fortune on his side. His mother happened to read a newspaper article about open tryouts for the St. Louis Cardinals in nearby Columbus, Ohio. Fate called and 17-year old Harvey answered. He and his dad set off for the tryouts. When they arrived at Red Bird Stadium (home of the Cardinals' farm club), he wasn't able to be seen the first day, because there were so many other young athletes hoping for the same chance. On the second day, the scout gave him a form that required him to check a box for his desired position. He checked infield, outfield and pitcher. The scout, Walter Shannon, said, "You can't play all three, son." Shannon took the form and scratched off infield and outfield. "Try pitching." No one knew then, the historical significance this suggestion would have.

Harvey threw 12 pitches during his tryout. They were good pitches, but Harvey caught the decision-makers' eyes for another reason. Harvey had a strong physical resemblance to another lefty

Cardinal pitcher, Harry 'the Cat' Brecheen (Brick-Keen). Although Harvey was smaller, he gave the scouts hopes of a smaller version of Harry the Cat. Harry had been the first lefthander in Cardinals history to win three games in a World Series, and had earned his nickname from his versatility as an outfielder. He had cat-like reflexes when it came to getting to the ball. Noting Harvey's smaller size, Shannon said, "We'll call him 'Harvey the Kitten'."

The windup came in 1947 when Harvey Haddix signed with the St. Louis Cardinals.

Shortly after signing with the Cardinals, Harvey was called up for the United States Army. The Cardinals kept 'The Kitten' nickname waiting for him when he returned from the service.

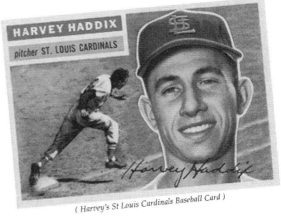

(Harvey's St Louis Cardinals Baseball Card)

YOU CAN GO HOME AGAIN

I first started my version of writing at the age of six. For a kid that age, it turns out I had a decent knack for poetry, which can be a blessing and a curse in the Bronx. In my grade school, they posted some of my poems in the halls of Waverly Avenue Elementary. I was even asked to read one over the loudspeaker system to the entire school on a Friday morning. "Who is the Sun?" was the name of the poem. At six years old, apparently I had the sun all figured out, well ahead of the modern scientists. Here is the poem as I remember it now:

Who is the Sun?

Is he a man with a gun and a belt?

If he gets angry will everything melt?

Does he control space?

Can he go anyplace?

All I know is we need the morning sun.

He starts the day for everyone.

Ok there you have it; I was six at the time.

Looking back, you could say I was always asking questions. I always wanted to know why something was, but I wanted real answers, not the usual made-up answers adults would tell kids. As a kid, your parents are required to give you bullshit answers to so many things. Let's call it 'P2,' or as I will refer to it from here as Parental Propaganda. My mother in particular was a propaganda machine. She could have been in the CIA!

Things my mother would say:

"If you make that face again it will freeze that way!" "It's funny until somebody gets hurt..." (I grew to agree with that one.) *"Don't drink the milk out of the container, or the whole house will get cooties." "Don't eat all the Yodels, or I'll start hiding them."* (Why did my mother buy Yodels if we weren't supposed to eat them?) *"Whatever you do just don't take out the BB gun. BB guns are dangerous!"* (I was never allowed to take out the BB gun. So why did they get me the BB gun in the first place? It made no sense.)

My father was just an illiterate asshole with a ton of misplaced anger, and certainly never hesitated using physical aggression. It was his way of problem solving. You'll cozy up to my wild ride with him as we roll through my family memoirs. I learned fairly early in life to stop listening to him at all. I became an expert at avoiding him at all costs. When his Green Blazer pulled in the driveway, I either walked out the backdoor and went to a friend's house or just headed straight up to my room and did homework. Thankfully, I had the right instincts. I observed other kids interact with their fathers and watched

(On my stoop, Bronx 1966)

fathers on television… no physical or verbal abuse. Our family life was more like the movie Raging Bull, rather than Brady Bunch or Leave it to Beaver. I saw other kids who were proud of their fathers and enjoyed spending time with them, while I was ashamed of mine.

I was very lucky to have my relationship with Pop, my maternal grandfather. He was the polar opposite of my father and our relationship had me wishing every day that he was my dad. If Pop was my dad, childhood would have been smooth sailing. Met games, playing catch and all the White Castles a kid could eat. One day, I realized my time growing up in the Bronx was dwindling as I heard my parents talking about moving to Long Island. From the city to the 'country' as it was called back then, I remember driving out to all of these strange towns. We would be busy looking at houses on Long Island every weekend. I didn't know why we were looking at houses, or why we wanted to move. I didn't know what the country was, or what it really meant. My concerns revolved around my daily trip to the candy store across the street and riding my bike to school. My candy store trips were almost always financed by my grandmother, who always slipped me money when my parents weren't looking. A two bedroom apartment in the Bronx seemed just fine to me. I didn't know from anything else. I had a

(On my stoop, Bronx 2013)

routine, I guess.

We did go upstate once to see Uncle Frank and Aunt Eleanor, which was my closest experience to being a kid out in the wilderness. They had a cool house that was more like a cabin, where we would catch frogs, salamanders, snakes and turtles. I remember going off with my cousins as if we were Huck Finn and friends, deep into the woods. Underneath the rocks and tree logs would be snakes, newts and salamanders. It was awesome; it took my mind off things. Here I was, a kid from the Bronx out in the deep woods in the middle of nowhere. I had no idea where I was, where I was going, or how to get back. It was thrilling, frightening and my first real sense of big adventure in a world I never knew existed. We captured wild creatures, put them in an old five gallon paint bucket and laughed and joked around the entire trip. When it was time to leave, we let all the creatures go, as my dad so lovingly reminded us that "We aren't starting a fucking zoo at our apartment! We have the Bronx Zoo right down the street!" That was true, but he never took us there. "Back to reality," I would be thinking. We also visited Aunt Helen and Uncle Dan in Freehold, New Jersey. Aunt Helen was my Godmother. My father said Uncle Dan was a "phony hooknose." I had no idea what a hooknose was and didn't ask. I figured I would get to the bottom of it someday, or maybe ask my mom. All I knew is that since the phrase began with 'phony', it couldn't have been that endearing.

Mom had a few very odd qualities of her own. When she was on the phone, my mother would speak in a totally different voice. My brother, Todd, and I later dubbed it, "The Aunt Helen Voice." My mom's voice would change depending on which friend or relative she was speaking with. One minute she would be yelling at us, using swear words in a thick Bronx accent. "Put your F@#*in' stuff away or you'll get a beating when your father gets home!" Then the phone would ring and we knew it was Aunt Helen, or even Aunt Maryann, depending on which voice we heard. It was the 1960's version of Madonna suddenly speaking with a British accent. Mom would incorporate an aristocratic, high-pitched voice, as if she just came back from vacationing in the Swiss Alps. I'd hear lots of bragging. We were doing this and buying that, and going here and going there.

Meanwhile, we weren't buying anything, or going anywhere. The only thing going on in our house was my father threatening to rip the phone out of the wall because the bill was too high from all the calls placed to my grandmother, my Aunt Helen and Aunt Mary-Ann. Between that and the constant threat to my Yodel supply, the lesson that was burned into my brain was:

Just because someone says something, it doesn't mean it's true. Even if that person is your own mother.

She would talk to Aunt Helen for what seemed like an eternity. Then my grandmother would call and it would be a totally different conversation and my mom would immediately return back to her regular voice. For the life of me, I couldn't figure this out. The phone bill would come each month and with it came the screaming, cursing and arguing with my dad. My father promised on numerous occasions that he was ripping the phone out of the wall. He would threaten this over and over again. The screaming and cursing would escalate, "I swear to god the next sixty dollar phone bill comes to this fuckin house, the mother fuckin phone is going to be ripped right out of the mother fuckin wall!" I kind of wanted to see this happen. After months and years of threatening, rip the thing out of the wall already!

Mean what you say! Say what you mean. A promise is a promise.

My father would ask my mother why she talked to her mother all day. At that time Mom didn't drive, so my father said he was getting her a bicycle so they could talk face-to-face. He said he was buying a bike with a basket so she could also get groceries. It would be cheaper. He would ask why she didn't call my grandmother collect. "Reverse the charges from now on," he said. Calling collect was a big thing back then, and many people reading this may not even know what that means. Collect calls are a thing of the past, but were quite popular when I was growing up. Collect, long distance, and pay phones. If someone called collect or long distance there was screaming and running through the house as if it was on fire, because they were big deals. "Stephen, you have a call LONG DISTANCE!!!" My father would call from a pay phone and before I could say hello, I'd hear, "Go get your mudda; I'm at a pay phone!" I'd scream, "Mommmmm.......dad's at a PAY PHONE!!!" A payphone was in the top three of alert colors. Let's put them in order:

Long Distance	*Red Alert*
Collect Call	*Orange Alert*
Pay Phone	*Yellow Alert*

This same phone bill scene would take place every month, like clockwork. I dreaded the arrival of the phone bill. It began with my Mom hiding it. We would watch my dad search for it. Then the yelling started, and escalated to screaming. These monthly occurrences were my first experiences with adults not following through with what they said. Now, as an adult myself, I see it all the time.

I call it "big hat, no cattle".

People just go on and on about all these things they are going to do, even saying they have already done them, when truthfully, it will never happen. It occurred to me that maybe it makes them feel better for a minute, or they don't think you will ever find out. It does damage to the person who believes these lies, or is counting on what was promised. One simple rule that will put you ahead of any class:

If you say you're going to do something, then do it.

If you can't do something, that's OK. Just say it. As Coach Knight, the legendary Indiana Coach, has taught me:

You are much better off saying no, and that you will try. Going from no to yes beats the hell out of going from yes to no every time.

As a six or seven year old, you really don't have a grasp for money, or what things cost. Your grasp of money is limited to opening birthday or Easter cards. Sometimes cards would have the coins inserted, or maybe, if it's your lucky day, a five dollar bill. To me, a five dollar bill was a month of pizza and candy at the deli across the street. Today, five dollars is nothing to kids! Here's the math: In my first year on Long Island, my friends and I would walk to Pizza Stop. A slice was $.25 and

(Pizza Stop, 25¢ a slice)

a fountain coke was $.20. Three slices of Pizza and a coke was $.95. Mom would give me a dollar and I would have a nickel change.

My father announced at breakfast one morning we were heading out to Long Island to go hunting for a house. I never thought house hunting could teach me so many things. I learned about life, real estate and the monetary system. That Friday, my grandmother came over to wish us well. Grandma had offered to stay at our apartment and watch me, but no dice. I was told I had to go. She brought a styrofoam cooler filled with snacks and candy for the trip. We packed up and drove due east on the Long Island Expressway, my father pretending to study his notes of prominent towns in which to buy. After we looked at a house, my father would add up the taxes, monthly payments and the "Litco" bill as he called it, even though the actual company name was Lilco (gas and electric). The more he calculated, the more he would whip himself into a frenzy. Yelling, yelling, and more yelling. He yelled about everything, from his job to his boss to the mutts and the hooknoses. I still didn't know what a hooknose was yet. He would go nuts on how much everything costs and how little he got paid from his job. He couldn't believe how expensive the houses were. After every house it would be the same song and dance. At this point I'm thinking that buying a house must really suck if it causes all this stress. My life as a kid was stressful enough as it was. This whole house thing was making us even more miserable. It was only after my father went nuts and then cooled down that he and my mom could actually talk about the house, the features, Stephen's room, Todd's room, a room if my grandmother came out, etc. Todd was three years younger than me. A few of the houses had beautiful yards and I thought I could play stickball there. It would be great to play in a backyard rather than the middle of the street like in the Bronx. The streets seemed not very busy like the Bronx, so even if you played in the street, you might have to move for a car only once in a while. In the Bronx, we would constantly have to stop the game for a passing car going down Van Nest Avenue. This realization made me think that moving might wouldn't be that bad. But wait a minute…I was only changing locations; I wasn't moving in with a different family.

We had many a Saturday and even a Sunday or two of intensive searching, haggling, pain and negotiations. In what seemed like an eternity of yelling, screaming and getting lost, we finally found 20 Hetty's Path in Farmingville. The search was over.

My personal highlights of house-hunting were all the times we got lost. I'd hear my mom say, "Junior, we are lost!" (My mom often referred to my father as Junior.) He would say we were fine. He knew exactly where we were, as he went turkey hunting years before right in this exact spot. It didn't matter what town we were in, that was his line and we never saw a single turkey. I never even saw him hunt. The rest of the family knew for certain we were lost when he would find a random person, roll down the window and yell out, "Hey old timer," if the guy was old, "hey fatso" if the guy was fat, or "stretch" if the person was tall. He called them these insulting names like they knew each other for years, but Old Timer, Fatso or Stretch would simply make a strange face and give him directions anyway. I could never understand it. If it was me I would have just walked away from the rude lunatic. He made me cringe and we got lost on every trip. Driving around like that made my brother and me hungry. If we were hungry, my mom would say she was hungry too. Dad would tell us to hold our horses or he would climb in the back seat and give us a beating. While he was driving? I'd love to see that!

Anyway, most of the time I just wanted to get out of the car so I could breathe fresh air again. Both of my parents chain-smoked the entire car ride. I would have my head out the back window like a curious German Shepherd making sure he wasn't headed for the dog pound. They would scare me and say that at any minute my head could be cut off by a tree. So I'd pull my head back in and breathe in the smoke. I think I was ahead of my time in fearing the deadly effects of second-hand smoke. Purchased for $17,500, our little haven off of exit 61 on the Long Island Expressway was a pristine suburban sanctuary.

Thirty years later, the neighborhood is shot—littered with pawn shops, laundromats, tattoo and piercing shops and the businesses with signs that read 'We Buy Gold for Cash'.

We weren't even moved in yet but I couldn't wait to be old enough to move out.

Our new home, a simple two-story colonial on a quarter acre of land, was situated precisely on the border of two towns, Farmingville and Centereach. If you lived on our side of the street, you went to Sachem schools, while the other side went to Middle Country Schools. A rivalry was firmly established long before we even moved in. Living across the street from Centereach, I had the pleasure of hearing my father say, "Cenner-ich". He left out the T that was put in place by whoever named the town. Somehow "each", a fairly simple word to pronounce, became "itch." He was so annoying! As we go on, I will more clearly define the vocabulary of **The Hand.** This was the nickname that Todd and I gave to my father. We called him The Hand because he put his hand up to his face when he spoke. Talking through his hand was a weird habit, but the least of my problems.

A little research showed that Centereach was originally known as Middle Village, because it sat directly in the Middle of Long Island. However, it was discovered that there was a town with the same name in upstate New York. Therefore it was changed to Centereach because it was easily reached from anywhere on Long Island, or the boroughs of New York City. I don't know how the town of Farmingville got its name. According to research, it has nothing to do with agriculture although judging from all the leaves I raked over the years, they had no problem growing trees. Farmingville is most famous for the 2004 documentary 'Farmingville', based on the tribulations of illegal immigrants.

When I moved to Farmingville in 1968 there were no illegal immigrants. Ninety-nine percent of the kids I went to school with were white. With the exception of Dave (probably not his birth name), the proprietor of our local Chinese restaurant, Hao-Po, everyone we knew was Caucasian. The only time you saw a non-white person in our town was when the Native American Indians drove around selling handmade redwood furniture from the back of their truck. They slowly drove around the neighborhood with the furniture stacked up on the back of a flat bed and would ring a cowbell to announce their presence.

One day my father decided we needed outdoor furniture. He yelled for me to get out there and stop the Indians, which I did. My family gathered shoulder-to-shoulder, like a soccer team trying to block a penalty kick, as my father negotiated. It was so embarrassing because my father called one of them "Geronimo" and the other, "Sitting Bull," as if they all knew each other in a past life of Cowboys and Indians. After about an hour of back-and-forth (including my father attacking their tribal heritage), a deal was made. Finally, off came the redwood. During lunch, we obediently listened to my father retell the scene we just witnessed. In his version, it grew into an epic tale of how my father divided and conquered them. He was boasting about how he got a great deal from Geronimo and how he robbed him and Sitting Bull. He went into specific detail on each piece of furniture he acquired for the family. They wanted a hundred and fifty for the sofa; he ended up getting it for fifty. He got a great deal, while they were probably out "robbing all the neighbors." He promised us the neighbors paid full price. My father boasted that the neighbors couldn't negotiate like him. He even went out later that day and bought a padlock for the gate to our back patio. He suspected the Indians may come back at nightfall and steal the furniture back. He was certain of it! He edified us about the term "Indian giver" and how its origins came from Indians

(The Redwood!)

selling redwood furniture to people, then going to each house during the night and stealing it back. Then the next day, they would sell the same furniture in a different neighborhood. He said it kept their overhead extremely low. After he proudly installed the padlock, every half hour he would look outside to make sure the furniture was still there, even though it wasn't even nightfall yet. He told us of what the Indians did to Custer in the "Battle of Little Big Horn." The Indians surrounded Custer and his troops, killing everyone. Then they took all of their scalps as souvenirs. I was shocked he knew anything about Custer, as I was certain that my father barely attended school. If he did attend, he was probably there just to beat up somebody. According to all the history books, Custer's scalp remained intact. Custer was an amazing man and brave General. After graduating last in his class at West Point, Custer went on to years of triumph with his 7th Cavalry, until being defeated at the Battle of the Little Bighorn. The victorious Sioux tribe did not take Custer's scalp or mutilate his body, as was their tradition. (They did this so the dead would not be able to get into Heaven.) Some historians argue that the Sioux left his body intact out of respect and admiration for the General, while others argue in favor for other reasons. But the facts are that Custer's body was allowed to be claimed by U.S. troops and given a proper burial, scalp and all. But my father stuck to his own version of the story – knowing better than historians or eyewitness accounts.

That's why my father said he always slept with one eye open. Personally, I was hoping Geronimo and Sitting Bull would come back and steal the furniture (it would have served him right) as long as they didn't take my scalp. They could have taken his scalp it wouldn't have bothered me. He even made our elderly beagle, Princess, sleep outside that night. He gave the dog specific instructions to bite any Indians coming for the redwood furniture. Since he was speaking through his hand, I doubt the dog knew what he was saying. I could barely make out what he was saying! You probably think I'm making some of this up. I wish! I'm really not—you can't make this stuff up. Just be glad you didn't live through it. Princess hated my father as much as I did. I thought about staying outside with Princess that night to keep her company, but then I started thinking that they might come back for the furniture, and scalp me. I figured I was safer in my bed. Throughout that night when Princess would cry, or scratch on the door, he would shoot down the stairs, roll up the Newsday and threaten Princess with a beating. The dog was no stranger to a beating just like the rest of us. Princess feared the rolled up newspaper as it was often the preamble to a beating. Then he told the dog to look out for the Indians and he pointed to his eye, and said "Watch!" like the dog could actually understand what he was saying.

The next morning, he was up early. I could tell, because I heard his morning routine with the usual horrible throat hacks and assorted other noises. I wonder if smoking four packs of Camels a day had anything to do with that. Then I heard the sliding glass door screech open. He was seeing if the furniture was still there. It was. He was victorious. Damn!

I made sure when I came downstairs that I acknowledged the furniture. "Dad, they didn't take the redwood, huh?" "The padlock probably saved us," he said. "Probably" I said. This was just another one of our great father-son talks. I think Princess had to endure three more nights outside until he finally gave up thinking the Indians were returning to take the furniture. But the padlock stayed. The worst part was that he wouldn't give anyone the combination to the padlock, not even my mother. The combination to the padlock was top secret. I couldn't even get my bike out of the back yard; I had to take it through the house out the front door, with my mother screaming and chasing me with a damp rag. A damp rag was her solution to everything. Broken leg? Damp rag. Polio? Chicken Pox? Damp rag. My mother always had a damp rag close by to wash or clean something. Once the redwood furniture was secure and the house had some more patio accoutrements, we started having some of the relatives out on the weekends. Out came all the hooknoses! The Costello family was ready to entertain, out in the country.

HARVEY HADDIX WINS
HIS FIRST WORLD SERIES

Harry "The Cat" Brecheen was the first pitcher in the history of baseball to win three games in a World Series, as his 1946 Cardinals outlasted Ted Williams and his mighty Red Sox. The entire 7 Game series would keep fans on the edge of their seats right up until the moment of Enos "Country" Slaughter's famous mad dash, which would ultimately bring Brecheen and his Cardinals to a dramatic World Series victory. It wouldn't be until 1960 that another World Series would again capture that type of excitement. This time it was Harvey Haddix pitching in Game 7 for the Pittsburgh Pirates. In the bottom of the ninth inning, a thunderous home run blast by Pirates Bill Mazeroski brought the mighty Yankees to their knees. After the game, the legendary Yankee Manager, Yogi Berra, gave the press a very early Yogi-ism. "We made too many wrong mistakes." Who would have imagined when "Harvey the Kitten" signed with the Cardinals, that he would have the greatest game ever pitched, along with a victory in Game 7 of the 1960 World Series? The scout's instincts were dead on. They should have nicknamed Harvey "The Tiger" as he won more games in his career than Brecheen, and snuffed out the mighty Yankees in the 1960 World Series.

Game 7 Thursday, October 13, 1960 at Forbes Field
PITCHERS:
NYY - Turley, Stafford (2), Shantz (3), Coates (8), Terry (8)
PIT - Law, Face (6), Friend (9), Haddix (9)
WP - Harvey Haddix (9)

	Yankees	at	Pirates	
	9		10	

	1	2	3	4	5	6	7	8	9	R	H	E
Yankees	0	0	0	0	1	4	0	2	2	9	13	1
Pirates	2	2	0	0	0	0	5	1	10	11	0	

While Brecheen was retiring Williams and Pesky, Harvey was passing out one-way tickets to the dugout, to the mightiest of Yankee heroes:

Mantle, Boyer, Richardson, Rizzuto, Berra, and Maris. This is the stuff that legends are made of and I am here to give Harvey his overdue recognition! The Yankees Empire of the early 60's was one of the most powerful hitting dynasties in the history of baseball and he shut them down. The first thing the Yankees did was fire Casey Stengel, like it was his fault! The following year, 1961, Harvey Haddix was a World Series Champion and I was born to Stephen and Florence Costello. Hooray!

I THOUGHT TO MYSELF, LET'S SEE YOUR A's AND B's YOU ILLITERATE ASSHOLE!

Farmingville, Long Island was 60 miles dead east of the Statue of Liberty. Of course, 'The Hand' mispronounced Farmingville as well. He left the G out, and called it "Farm-in-vulle." If you corrected him, you were threatened with a beating. So in 1968 we were officially residents of Farm-in-vulle. I grew up at the end of the Commie Era, and the beginning of the Hippie Era. My dad said anyone with long hair, a colorful shirt, or a bright idea was a hippie, and anyone who was anti-government was a commie. Of course, my dad was anti-government, but that didn't make him a commie. That hypocrisy made sense to him. The State Farm Insurance neighbor was a Hippie, according to dad. My dad said they were a whole family of "reefer smoking hippies". He said he could smell the pot from our front yard, but nobody else ever smelled anything. Could it be any worse than the nicotine cloud that floated over our entire house? Pot might be a welcome change.

When I got older, those neighbors asked me to baby-sit a few times. My dad said you don't baby-sit for hippies. They'll give you LSD and you'll go on a long trip and never return. He said the father was a half a fag and would try to grab my nuts when I wasn't looking. I didn't really believe my dad but I didn't want the guy grabbing my nuts either, so I played it safe.

Without experiencing these things first-hand, you may find some of this funny. Believe me, there was nothing funny about it at the time. And it was this same guy, with all of his historical misrepresentations, inability to pronounce names correctly and screwed-up world views who would pass judgment on my report card, every quarter. A week before it came out, I was already stressed over the report card process. I always got mostly A's with a B here or there. The teacher's comments were always positive. We would finish dinner, and then my mother would trumpet the announcement. "Junior...Stephen's report card came today." She called him Junior because his dad was Stephen Costello as well. His dad ran away when my dad was ten years old. I was nowhere near that lucky. He always said the same thing, "Let's see that there report card." To my book editor, that sentence doesn't need editing; that's just how he said it. The ritual would begin with him looking at the report card up and down. It seemed like an eternity while I sat there frightened to death with my palms sweating. A bad report card equaled a beating, no question. Then he would say, "What happened here?" (It was a B, for God's sake!) I thought to myself, let's see your A's and B's you illiterate asshole! I would tell him that I would get an A next time, and the show would go on. I never had anything that even resembled a bad grade, but he had to make a song and dance out of it anyway. He would say, "you better get all A's or you'll wind up being a truck driver like me." I hated the report card ritual and detested him even more afterward. The thing I loved most about school was he wasn't there. I would have taken night classes if they let me. By fourth or fifth grade, something occurred to me. The only way this guy could stare that long at a report card is if he probably didn't know how to read.

LONG ISLAND LIVING -
FAR FROM PARADISE ISLAND

It is a bit of a transition for a kid to move from the city to the country. I no longer walked one block to St. Dominic's; I had to take a bus to school. The bus situation was especially daunting. I waited on the corner of Radburn Drive for this big yellow bus to take me to some far-away place. Again, I had more questions than answers.

"Where was it taking me?"

"Would I get there okay?"

"What bus would I go home on?"

The bus is a frightening thing to a six-year old that always walked to school. As it turns out, I was worried over nothing. After a day or two I had the hang of it and was fine. In an early version of this book, I had a section on worrying. My book doctor, Doug, told me to take it out of the book. Too bad book doctor, my book…my ideas! I have the final vote. So here goes: it's important to not worry. If worrying actually solved anything, then I would be all for it.

The things you should worry about generally catch you by surprise. You never even got the chance to worry about them in the first place. So don't worry, be happy!

Anyway, I met three other kids at that bus stop—Peter D'Amico, Jimmy Randazzo, and Mark Hertzovitz. Over time, they would become my best friends. Most of my childhood memories include them in one way or another. They probably have no idea the important role they would play in my formative years, adolescence, and ultimately, the decisions that I would make throughout the next forty years of my life. You have your first friends, and your best friends. These guys were both in one way or another.

I grew up on Hetty's Path. Peter and Jimmy lived next door to each other on Arden Lane and Mark's house was past Arden Lane, on Grendon Lane. Everyone lived in a similar cookie cutter Levitt house, which was cool in the fact that we more or less all had the same size houses and back yards. Everyone had the same things.

I moved from the Bronx, Peter and Jimmy came from Queens and Mark came from Brooklyn. That sums up Long Island's demographic. People who wanted to get out of the boroughs would move and settle into different Long Island towns. After school, we would take turns going to each other's houses and playing Wiffle ball, football, basketball, ping pong, and every other imaginable sport. When it got dark, we moved right into board games and card games. Peter was my match in Scrabble. I was quite the Scrabble player, but Peter was every bit as good. He grew up to be a Doctor of Psychology, so it's no surprise he was a scrappy Scrabble player as a kid. Sometimes his mom would play as well. She was Scrabble-savvy as well. I always took comfort in being at the D'Amico's house because his dad was mild-mannered and everyone seemed to get along. They treated me well there.

The D'Amico family didn't have the yelling, screaming and battling that always went on in my house. They would always talk things out. I didn't know what normal family life was. From 1969 to 1974 every Friday night I would sit three feet from the

(*Peter, Me, Mark, during an intense championship scrabble game* " *I think I won this one* ")

television and watch the Brady Bunch. All week long I looked forward to the Brady Bunch, and had a huge crush on Marsha. All the Brady kids all seemed to get along. Each week, the family humorously solved the crises of six kids growing up together. Robert Reed (Mike Brady) wasn't ripping the phone out of the wall, and you never saw anybody get a beating. He wasn't handing out tire irons to the kids to chase the bug guys. The Brady kids weren't handed a rake or a black bag to put the leaves in. I remember wishing I could be a Brady. I would have loved to live there for just a week. Watching the Brady Bunch was a mesmerizing half hour for me.

Back in school, one thing that I was certain about was that my three friends were not fond of my poems. One day they would say that I wrote like a fairy and the next they would say they were certain that my mother wrote my poems. As you would imagine, this upset me. I tried to reason with them, requesting that we decide on one method of emasculation. I either write like a fairy, or my mother wrote my poems—they couldn't have it both ways. I stayed firm on this. One day we were hanging out in my back yard and my friends all had big smiles on their faces. It turns out that they all brought their own poems with them. They couldn't stop laughing before they even got started. I knew right away I was in for trouble. Peter read his first.

"Roses are red
Violets are blue
When I need a poem for school,
My mother writes one too!"

Everyone cracked up. Then came Jimmie's, then Mark's. They just didn't understand me. Or maybe they understood me too well. The crazy thing is that nobody can get under your skin the way your friends can. I always secretly wondered if they were really my friends. Where is the friend stuff you see on TV? Shouldn't they be offering encouragement and support? So, I rarely brought up my poetry around my friends. I became a closet poet. We could only taunt each other for so long, because everything we did took four people. Stickball, football, basketball, you name it. If I was mad at them, they were one guy short and couldn't do anything. They would apologize to make me feel better, but it was an apology in kids-speak. At the age of eight I began to understand leverage.

"Come on, we need you for Wiffle ball."

"NO!"

"We won't say your mother wrote your poems."

"NO!"

"We won't say the only thing your mother cooks is frankfurters."

"NO!"

"We won't say you have a sunken chest."

Finally, I would give in and we would all laugh and go outside to play. The good thing about us is that we were equal opportunity— everybody took a beating. The walk to catch the bus was always an adventure. With roller hockey extremely popular, at any minute you could get "Bill Groll'd." Okay, I need to explain this. The four of us would be walking to the bus stop. If one of us was daydreaming or not paying attention, somebody would yell "Bill Groll!" and the person not paying attention would get slammed into the sharp, green sticker bushes, while the other three laughed. The sticker bushes not only hurt, but had red berries that would get red gooey stuff all over your clothes. My sunken chest and I were not fond of this painful ritual. At least at the roller rink my guard was up for this stuff. However, when you're worrying about catching the bus and talking about the Mets game last night, you're just not ready to be sneak-attacked by your own friends. A trip into the sticker bushes meant you're starting the day in the nurse's office.

My Bill Grolls were never as good as the other guys. I wasn't as strong as the other three and I didn't weigh as much. I was actually interested in getting to school and learning something. My attempts at Bill Grolling consisted of bouncing off one of my friends without knocking them anywhere near the sticker bushes. Finally, I just started walking in the middle of the street.

(Bill Groll (White) of The New York Chiefs takes out number 40 on the San Francisco Bombers.)

THE GREATEST GAME EVER PITCHED

I think part of the reason I am writing about Harvey Haddix and his historic feat is that so few people are aware of it in the first place. I alluded to this in the first chapter. Believe it or not, the only people who saw Harvey pitch that night were at the game. That's because the local TV station, KDKA, chose to show a speech of then Vice-President Richard Nixon instead of the Braves vs. Pirates game! Because of this, no footage of the game exists. On top of that, three decades later there was a minor rule change that strikes his no-hitter from the record books. Harvey's perfect game history evaporated like water on a hot griddle. Ask your baseball-loving friends who Harvey Haddix is. There's a big chance they've never heard of him, sad, but true.

OK Harvey, I'm starting to feel the pressure now. We're no longer talking about first grade poems; we're talking about a written explanation of your accomplishment, folded into my screwy childhood. *I'm putting forth a detailed account that holds up to scrutiny and when the dust settles, your place in history will be rightly restored—with the proper fanfare.*

On that misty, historic, magical night in Milwaukee, fighting off flu-like symptoms, Harvey Haddix delivered a poetic performance—a performance that has still never quite found its rightful place in history. A performance never replicated by any pitcher since then. Don Hoak, your third baseman and good friend,

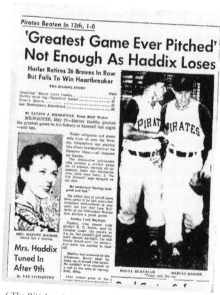

(*The Pittsburgh Press - May 27, 1959 article from the day after the Haddix perfect game*)

seemed to be the catalyst for things starting to unravel for you. Surprisingly, you said later that you hadn't even realized it was a perfect game, as you thought you "may have walked a few fellas along the way." Don didn't feel great about you losing the game and later said, "I made some errors before that, and made a few more after that." I may have gone through my entire life being a baseball fan who was oblivious of your accomplishment, but now, I'm all about it. Your name should be mentioned with Jim Bunning, Don Larsen, Cy Young, and David Cone. Not Ron Robinson, Milt Pappas, and Hooks Wiltse. Your record belongs back in the books. You aren't "Hard Luck Harvey the Kitten" to me. Win or lose, no one will ever pitch 12 perfect innings ever again.

POETRY AND ME

In second grade I get my first big literary break. One of my poems gets published in McCall's Magazine. I broke my rule of telling my friends about the poetry stuff and brought the magazine on the bus. Not a good idea. They taunted me and called me Mary Jane, Mary Ann and Annie. The bus ride home meant more girls' names they thought of throughout the day. My friends would tell you that when my mom wasn't writing my poems for me, she was mailing them to magazines. I sometimes wonder how kids survive. Kids are certainly more brutal than adults. My friends were nothing short of ruthless. They knew exactly what to say to get under your skin.

But I continued writing poetry. With practice, they were getting better. My mom and I met with a publisher about creating a collection (I believe it was Doubleday). They ended up sending a rejection letter that said they loved the poems, but felt children would not appreciate poetry written by someone their age. That made perfect sense to me, based on my friends' reactions. So really, only my mother was disappointed. Maybe I was a little disappointed also. My father was happy about it, because I could stop being a child prodigy and go back to weekend child-slave, raking the entire yard before I could do anything else. There were regular leaves, and pine needles. Pine needles are in a totally different category, because they would always slip through the rake. After I'd finish raking the leaves, my father would conduct an intense inspection. He'd see all the leaves were gone, and then say, "You're not finished till all *these here* pine needles are gone." So back to the yard I'd go. A few years later I figured out the lawn mower would suck them all up, so I waited for him to go somewhere and then mow the lawn. Goodbye pine needles! While other kids were jumping in gigantic piles of leaves with their friends and family, I was putting them in black bags and lining them up on the curb. It occurred to me that…

I was my father's son, but I was not my father.

My father would storm into my room on a Saturday morning, wake me up and demand "What are you doing today?" As any eight-year-old would reply, "I'm not sure dad, I just woke up." He would announce "I know exactly what you're doing today, YOU'RE DOING YAAAAAAAAARDWORK!!!!" His Bronx-Italian accent made it hardly seem like English, but the meaning was crystal clear. I was screwed for the day. It sucked being the son of a total asshole, but I was too little to fight him and not yet able to out-smart him. I didn't have a plan of escape, so I'd go find my rake. Raking leaves is a mundane task, but it gives you piles of time to think. So while I gathered up the leaves, I thought about all the big stuff: being a newspaper editor, pitching in college, dating a pretty girl, having a cool car, and playing professional baseball one day.

Your dreams are your dreams and they have no deadlines.

My father could not steal my dreams from me. *So inside the big black leaf bags would go the leaves with my dreams, and I put my thoughts into those bags like a letter in a bottle*—I would daydream while raking. We were close to putting a man on the moon, which was an exciting time. In the evenings I would sit in the back yard and just look up at the sky. I couldn't fathom that we were sending a space ship with astronauts up there. Fast-forward four decades later. I have a colleague, Zak Karow, who is an absolute encyclopedia about every topic. A true know it all, he has the answer no matter what the question. I happened to ask him to complete a task for me, and followed up my request with, "Forty years ago we put a man on the moon, so this task should be doable." Zak responded, "How do you even know we went to moon?" That statement stopped me in my tracks, and inspired me to do a little research on conspiracy theories. Truthfully, I am now certain we never went to the moon. For right now we'll call that 'Book Number 2'. Thanks to Zak, I'm quite obsessed with this notion now and have viewed the "Some Angry Astronauts" video a hundred times.

As a kid I loved the dead of winter. The leaves were gone and the only yard work was occasional snow removal. Peter, Jimmy and Mark would come over with shovels. The three of us would make quick work of my driveway, and then head to the houses that didn't have shoveling age kids. We skipped the hippie next door as none of us wanted our nuts grabbed. We would get ten bucks a driveway, and up to twenty bucks if the driveway was extra big. Gigantic ones were forty bucks, according to Mark. Mark always did our negotiating. The days of shoveling snow taught me a little about business, and a little about myself. I wasn't afraid to go outside and nearly freeze to death to make a few bucks.

Later, I not only went on to pitch in college, but pitched in the most important game in the history of our school. We beat Evansville University, our cross-town rivals, for the first time in two decades. So, perhaps my dreams were able to escape those many bags of leaves, like a genie escaping his bottle. I remember standing on the pitcher's mound that day saying "Wow, here you are…what the hell?!" I had come so far from my back yard. I had come so far from my father calling me an idiot and belittling me. The only yelling came from fans at the game. I would have given anything for Pop to have been able to watch just one inning or even one pitch. I played within myself that day, and kept the strong hitters off balance with a combination of changeups and curveballs. It felt like little league all over again, and I was unhittable. Five strong innings, then my relief pitcher came in and closed out the game. Some days define you and for me, that was one of those days.

I was an adolescent at the time of the Watergate scandal. The investigatory prowess of Woodward and Bernstein made quite an impression on me. By the time I was in college, I had the ability to combine my athletics with a touch of investigative reporting. That ultimately led to the resignation of our basketball coach and the head of the food service. After that, I wrote a series of articles calling for our school's independence. This too, became a reality. Our school went from merely an annex of Indiana State University, to the University of Southern Indiana. More dreams escaping those bags of leaves!

UNIVERSITY of SOUTHERN INDIANA

(Be true to your school)

41

WHAT DO HARVEY HADDIX AND
WILT CHAMBERLAIN HAVE IN COMMON?

Okay Harvey, I'll tell you. I am in the sports marketing business now and consider myself a bit of a sports historian. As someone who prides himself on knowing a tremendous amount about the game and its history, you had totally escaped my radar. Now it's time to share with the rest of the world, your tremendous feats that somehow disappeared like the sun over the horizon on a forgettable day.

As we go along, I'll be sure to fill you in on the meandering path of my life and we will definitely cover the meandering path of yours. Yours led to the greatest game ever pitched, three All Star games, and two spectacular wins in the 1960 World Series. By the way, Major League Baseball re-televised that great game from 1960.

This is from Business Wire, December 13, 2010:

"PARIS & HOLLYWOOD--(BUSINESS WIRE)--Technicolor (Euronext Paris: TCH) (NYSE: TCH) announced it has worked with MLB Network, Major League Baseball's 24-hour cable TV network, to provide restoration-remastering of the sound and picture of the historic Game 7 of the 1960 World Series between the New York Yankees and Pittsburgh Pirates from the only known source in existence – five 16mm film reels found in late entertainer Bing Crosby's wine cellar. The original broadcast of the game will be televised December 15 on MLB Network at 8:00 p. m. ET, the first time the game will be seen on television since it was played more than 50 years ago. "

Millions of people who did not realize you won two games in that series, now know. The re-airing of the game was a huge success. The mighty Yankees were in such shock that day! Johnny Blanchard told me himself that Mickey Mantle cried in the locker room and Casey Stengel was fired for losing, despite having one of the best Yankee teams ever assembled.

Spending time with John Sterling recently, he mentioned that Casey thought the real reason that he was fired was the fact that he was turning 70. He felt that they were putting him out to pasture. Johnny Blanchard also told me if they played the 1960 Pirates again in the World Series, they would win 99 out of 100 times...but I'm sure you would disagree, Harvey. Adding insult to injury, they made Bobby Richardson the World Series Most Valuable Player, and the Yankees didn't even win! In the history of the World Series, only once in 85 years has the losing team been awarded the Most Valuable Player. They didn't think of giving it to you Harvey, or even Bill Mazoroski.

The Wikipedia entry for the summary of the 1960 World Series doesn't even mention Harvey Haddix, but it does state how mighty the Yankees were...and they didn't even win the series!

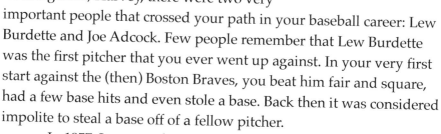

(Painting of Harvey Haddix
by RebeccaBarra.com)

Looking back, Harvey, there were two very important people that crossed your path in your baseball career: Lew Burdette and Joe Adcock. Few people remember that Lew Burdette was the first pitcher that you ever went up against. In your very first start against the (then) Boston Braves, you beat him fair and square, had a few base hits and even stole a base. Back then it was considered impolite to steal a base off of a fellow pitcher.

In 1957, Lew and the Milwaukee Braves (the Braves franchise moved to Milwaukee in 1953) did to the Yankees what you would later accomplish in the 1960 World Series. Lew Burdette, with Hank Aaron, of course, defeated a Yankee powerhouse that had won the 1956 World Series over the Dodgers. Lew stood tall on the mound inside Yankee Stadium, beating the Yankees in the seventh game of the World Series. 54,000 well-dressed Yankee fans quickly turned angry and depressed, when a sizzling line drive from Moose Skowron scorched the leather of Eddie Matthew's glove for the final out.

The Milwaukee Braves would win their first and only World Series title. 1957 was a storybook year as Joe Adcock, Lew Burdette and Hank Aaron would all get their first and only World Series rings. Just like you in 1960, your World Series ring would come at the expense of the New York Yankees – a special victory that comes along with being an underdog. But neither of you could escape the harm of those free cigarettes; Lew succumbed to lung cancer, and you to emphysema. By the time you guys learned the real deal about smoking, it was far too late.

YOU WANT TO TAKE THE
WIFFLE BALL FROM THE KIDS?

During the warm summer months, we played Wiffle Ball pretty much every single day. It was easy enough to re-create Shea Stadium on our street. Peter, Jimmy, Mark and I made boundaries, deliberating the way kids do. The corner of my house had a flat street and each neighbor had a fence to designate right and left fields. They were far enough away that a home run was a respectable distance. Home plate was a paper plate weighed down with a rock big enough to keep it from blowing away. First base and third base were trees that you grabbed with your hands and the fence along my house served as the foul line. It was perfect.

Someone told me many years later that Wiffle Ball was invented in the early 1950's. With the seriousness of our games, we were probably some of the earliest pros. Generally, we would start at 11 in the morning, play until lunch (frankfurters of course) and then play some more. Then we'd jump in the pool and play tag. The two safety ladders were 'safe'. On the

(Me, Peter, Jimmy, Mark, and some unknown kid)

really hot days, one of the greatest feelings was a running plunge into the pool with all of our clothes on. The hot summer sun would dry us just in time for another round of dramatic belly-flops for round 2 at our own Shea Stadium.

One particular day was rife with left field home runs, meaning the Wiffle Ball went over our neighbor's fence more than usual. To our dismay, Mr. Santori came out, yelled at us and confiscated the ball. Game over. With nothing else to do, I went back home where everything seemed the same as usual, on the surface. My father was sitting at the dining room table still in his Consolidated Freightways shirt. But on this particular night my father was unusually salty. Someone was screwing him out of something or another, building him up to a dinner time tirade. I tried to eat my food and not make any eye contact. Then my father asked the magic question.

"How was Wiffle Ball today?"

After a few seconds of deliberation, I explained that the game had ended abruptly when Mr. Santori had taken the ball. He immediately launched into a rage and instructed me and my brother, Todd, to follow him. I guess he needed witnesses. He stomped across the street and pounded on the door until Mrs. Santori answered. "What's the matter Steve?" asked Mrs. Santori. "Where's Ralph? Where's that rotten, miserable, hooknose bastard?" he shouted, pushing past her and going right inside the house. The next thing I know we are all inside the Santori house and he has his hands around Mr. Santori's throat. Dad is banging Mr. Santori's head against the wall, yelling and screaming, "Where's that fuckin' Wiffle Ball!?" "Where's that fuckin' Wiffle ball - you want to take a Wiffle Ball from kids!?!?"

Dad screamed this over and over. Mr. Santori could have used the inchworm guys right now. Mrs. Santori is screaming, his kids are crying and I am too scared to even feel embarrassed. I'm trying to shield my brother from seeing the brutality and finally, Mr. Santori (now bleeding) just barely escapes my father's clutches and disappears into another room.

Poor Mr. Santori, he didn't even have the courage to come back. He just rolled the Wiffle Ball out into the hallway. My father picked up the ball, handed it to me and the three of us headed back to our house. "That's what you do when some motherfucker takes something that belongs to you," he proudly announced, still breathing heavily from his efforts.

"You beat his head against the fuckin' wall 'til he gives it back!"

"You're crazy!" My mother scolded when my father bragged when he returned home. "You're an animal, Junior! How could you? The guy's wife is my best friend! Theresa's my best friend, Steve!"

"All you women do is coffee klatch anyway," my father said, dismissing my mother. Unfortunately, that is one of the memories from my childhood that will never go away. Forty years later, it still haunts me. It was difficult to watch. I often think I should have kept my mouth shut, and just bought another Wiffle Ball at Woolworths. We didn't see Mrs. Santori for a few summers after that, and when the ball went on his property, he simply threw it back to us. He was now living in fear like the rest of us. Join the club, it's not that exclusive.

BABE? ROGER? HANK? MARK? BARRY?

A dream of mine when I started this book was to speak with Hank Aaron, one-on-one, about the famous Harvey Haddix game. Much to my delight, he agreed to spend some time with me talking about you, Harvey, and the day you quieted his team's powerful bats for almost 13 innings, including his. By now, I had been fortunate enough to meet with Hank many times. There is something very intimidating about him. As the greatest natural Home Run hitter in the history of baseball, I was more than excited; I was nervous. I idolized Hank as a child, and along with Tommie Agee and Muhammad Ali, he was one of my all-time heroes. I collected his baseball cards, for god sakes.

The acceptance of this particular invitation was very special. One of my colleagues, Eric Levy, is very close with Hank and Hank is a very hard man to get close to, trust me. After about four years, Eric tells me that he has good news – Hank has told Eric he really likes me. I don't know when or where Hank decided this and I didn't care. Just the thought that Hank Aaron decided that I was important enough in his life to be liked or disliked was cool all by itself. I mean, who the hell am I? *Over time, one of the things that I have learned is that people like people who know their stuff. People also like people that are not afraid to say 'I don't know'. It's not a crime to not know everything.*

It's not that hard to out-know people.

I like to know my stuff and I love to listen. Whenever Hank would tell me stories, I was just proud he thought enough of me to tell me the stories; I didn't need to tell him any of my own. If I really wanted to tell stories, I could tell Hank's stories to my tennis guys on Saturday mornings. They would hang on every word. I knew Hank and they now knew a guy that was close to Hank. That's how it works. Hank liked Tommie Agee a lot and he knew I was close to Tommie. He knew that I knew everything about the five hall of fame players that came from Mobile, Alabama. Five is extraordinary, since the only two cities that produced more are New York and Chicago.

MY GRANDFATHER STEPPED UP TO BAT

My favorite thing to do was pitch in front of my grandfather. James Angley, my grandfather, was the greatest man I ever knew, hands down. My grandfather was the guy in my corner, and a man that made a tremendous difference in my life. On game days, I would put on my uniform and wait on the front lawn for Pop. I would be sure to do this super

(Mom with Pop when she married "The Hand")

early and play catch with my friends, before my father would start thinking up yard work ideas. I always played better when Pop was at a game, as I wanted to impress him. Truth be told, my three years with the St. Margaret's Indians, my pitches were practically unhittable. I started every All-Star game and the other teams' coaches would count my innings, as pitchers were only allowed seven innings per calendar week. My father didn't like the other coaches counting my innings. He would go to their dugout and tell the coach the next thing being counted would be his broken bones. My father was big and scary and in those days you had street law…you didn't call the police for that type of stuff.

In 1969, when I was eight years old, Pop took me to my first Mets game. It was unbelievable. A day of great seats, hot dogs, autographs, batting practice and cheers. Nothing could get the smile off my face! Pop said he got the tickets from fat John Koehler who worked for Newsday, who got them from Joe Donnelly the sportswriter. I was at Shea Stadium with Pop on a sun drenched day with a hot dog and a coke. That's why you can't kill baseball. Baseball will survive scandals, steroids, strikes and salaries. It's a great distraction in a crazy world. A memory of a kid and his grandpa that's just as strong forty years later. Baseball is powerful. It's not easy for just any sport to become the national pastime. When I played baseball, I was always filled with wonder. How did they know how far apart to put the bases? How did they know the distance from the mound to the plate? Why was it elevated? Was Bob Gibson that good that they had to lower it? I wanted to know! Throughout the development of the game there was plenty of trial and error with base distance and pitcher's mound height, resulting in the game that's played today. Note: Let's take a timeout here to discuss who really invented baseball. Surprise…it was **not** Abner Doubleday! The invention of baseball is credited to Alexander Joy Cartwright, after the game we know today evolved from cricket in the 1800's. Side note: baseball has no timeouts, and baseball is the only major sport without a clock.

Back to the game with me and Pop. The Mets played the Padres. Pop tipped the usher. Phil Niekro, up against Jerry Koosman, hit a home run. After the game, Pop dropped me off at home, and then drove all the way back home to the Bronx. That meant he drove around seven hours that day, just for me. Pop was a truck driver like my father and occasionally would let me spend the day with him on his truck. Not a day goes by that I don't think of Pop and I think he would be pretty happy at how things turned out for me.

Your accomplishments, big or small, are hollow, when they can't be shared by others.

(Mine will always be somewhat hollow,
as they can't be shared with Pop.)

RECORDS MADE OR BROKEN
SHOULD NOT BE ALTERED

Your wife and I would have to agree, Harvey, that you somewhat played on borrowed time. Getting shot in the head by a spray of shotgun pellets at the age of five could have finished you off, but it didn't. Had you not gone out that day sporting one of those leather aviator helmets, it may have been the end for you, and this story. It's a good thing your mom had such a keen eye for fashion. From all accounts, you were a better person than a pitcher and that's what really counts. I've talked with plenty baseball players and I've yet to find a single one who says you weren't a great guy. Ralph Kiner, Whitey Herzog, Fritz Peterson, Hank Aaron and Don Larsen all offered to help with me with this book and tell me about you. I was with John Sterling recently, who is a tremendous baseball historian. As we were chatting about you, he expressed his outrage that your perfect game plus three more innings is not officially recognized by baseball. Who took away your perfect game? It was Fay Vincent, who was the Major League Baseball Commissioner from 1989 to 1992.

(Me, Don, Yogi, Press Conference for Don Larsen's Perfect Game Jersey)

What the hell was he doing as the MLB's Commissioner, anyway? Tons of experience? Hell No! He spent time on the Securities and Exchange Commission, was an entertainment lawyer and was a Vice Chairman for Coca Cola and Columbia Pictures. This is not a guy who was qualified to rule on statistics of baseball accuracy. So…how did Fay Vincent become MLB's eights commissioner? It turns out that he was a close friend of MLB's seventh Commissioner, Bart Giamatti. Seven years before he became involved in MLB, Vincent was booted from Columbia pictures (possibly because of expensive decisions he made about the film Ishtar) and went on to negotiated Giamatti's MLB contract. This put him in position for a sweetheart deal. Somebody explain to me how do you go from an attorney negotiating a contract, to being your client's Deputy Commissioner, and then successor? I guess he learned that kind of stuff from his time at the Securities and Exchange Commission. But after three years as Commissioner, the owners gave him a no-confidence vote, and he had no choice but to resign.

During his controversial tenure, Vincent tried banning pitcher Steve Howe for drug problems and attempted to keep Kenny Rogers out of the All-Star game for wigging out on a camera man. (Kenny Rogers would go on to throw a perfect game on July 28, 1994 against the California Angels.) The Fay Vincent era in baseball was nothing more than a three-year joke. As a matter of fact, Major League Baseball left the position vacant for the next six years (1992-1998). This articulated that they would rather have nobody, than have Fay Vincent.

FREE CIGARETTES...SMOKE NOW, DIE LATER

In addition to the famous baseball players who wanted to talk about you, Harvey, there's one more VIP who has a say in your story. I woke up today and decided to see if I could find your lovely wife, Marcia. Surprisingly, I found her quickly. I dialed nervously and when she answered, I was definitely caught off guard. I guess I didn't expect her to answer. She immediately put me at ease and she could tell I knew my stuff about you. We spoke for quite a while and she mentioned a previous book that had been written about your life. The best she could say was, "the book was horrible." The two things that seemed to bother your wife the most was that the book had so many incorrect details, and the author or publishers never consulted with the family. For this book, my goal is to get it right. I made a promise to Marcia that this path with be filled with objectivity and factual information. One of my favorite expressions is this: "The truth is your friend".

I am a staunch believer that everything happens for a reason. On May 29th, 2010, about an hour after I wrote the first three pages of this book, Roy Halladay pitched a perfect game, offering divine intervention already. Since only 21 perfect games were thrown in the last hundred years and I've attempted three books in the past forty-four, I estimate that all of this, at best, is a million-to-one coincidence. *(Editor's note: on May 25, 2014, during the final edit of this book, Josh Beckett of the LA Dodgers threw his career first no-hitter!)*

The day I began writing this book, a perfect game was pitched.

So the next morning Marcia and I are on the phone again, and she's providing the inside scoop. She told me you didn't start smoking until you got to the big leagues, but only because RJ Reynolds put a carton of Camels in everyone's locker. How thoughtful of them. Bastards! A few things we didn't learn in history class about cigarettes:

In 1942 Brown and Williamson claimed that Kool's kept your head clear and protected you from colds…seriously. Lucky Strike, Chesterfield and Camels all came with a physician's recommendation and promoted great health benefits, including prevention of throat scratchiness. This was followed by a new invention lauded as a tremendous health protector from Kent cigarettes - the Micronite filter.

What was it made of? Asbestos! Go figure. Within four years, Kent figured out that the Micronite filter really wasn't the greatest health protector in history and discontinued it. Now you can't even find the word Micronite on spell check.

Today, most people are fully aware of the dangers of smoking. Back in your day, Harvey, you had no idea that it would lead to your death. Babe Ruth, Lou Gehrig, Ted Williams and Joe DiMaggio all were spokespeople for the tobacco industry. Sadly, your wife misses you and she wanted me to know that you really only smoked about a pack or two a day. Give or take. The day of the perfect game, you had a cigarette before every inning and as your superstition dictated, you had Dick Groat light them for you. Don Larsen had a similar superstition. He had a cigarette after every inning, except for the last one when Yogi Berra jumped into his arms – giving fans one of the greatest baseball pictures of all time.

Harvey's idea was that if he lit the first one he had to light them all. It's frightening to realize the grip the tobacco industry had on baseball and how many children started smoking in an attempt to emulate their heroes. But Harvey would be glad to know you can't even light a cigarette in a baseball stadium today. I imagine that today, very few baseball players smoke but that problem has been replaced with steroids, HGH and PEDs. I guess that stuff can kill you, too.

So finally, I have my sit down with Hank Aaron, and I am very nervous. Normally, very few things make me nervous. I am speaking one-on-one to one of the greatest Hall of Fame baseball players of all time, and to my delight, it seems like he is also looking forward to the conversation. As I sit next to him, I accidentally knock his coat to the floor. So, this is how our conversation starts: "Steve, did you just knock my coat on the floor?" "Sorry!" I sheepishly pick up Hank's coat and brush it off. I hang it back on the chair, and get a bit anxious. He says, "So you're writing a book, Steve? What about?"

Now Hank already knows what the book is about because Eric told him, and I knew that.

"I'm writing about Harvey Haddix's perfect game. I know you played in it and I was hoping that you could provide some details. Do you remember that game, Hank?" The guy played in 3,298 games to be exact, so I really don't know what to expect, but Hank is amazing in every way and this situation is no exception. His recollection blows me away. It was as if he played the game the night before. "Oh yeah, I remember it very, very well," said Hank (the second 'very' gave me chills). "We came back from a long road trip; I think it was eight games. It started out on the west coast." (They were in San Fran and Philly…Hank was on the money.)

"We got in late and we were very tired because our flight had been delayed. Then when I woke up it looked like rain. The sky was dark and it looked like it was about to pour anytime. I called the clubhouse a few times and nobody picked up. So I just drove down to the stadium normal time. Harvey was throwing hard – no, not hard, let's just say hard enough with real good control. He was a real little skinny guy. The game went on and we just never got to him. Then we were all getting really tired. I remember the bottom of the 13th, I think Don Hoak made a throwing error, they intentionally walked me and then Joe Adcock hit a ball in between two fences. It was a home run but I thought it was a double and Joe passed me on the bases. So instead of a 3-0 game, it ended one nothing. Lou Burdette went the whole way for us. He refused to come out of the game as long as Harvey was still in there."

Okay, for an aspiring writer and devoted baseball fan, it doesn't get any better than that. So now reverting back to my inner Woodward and Bernstein, I start with the cigarette questions. "Did you know Harvey died from smoking? He never smoked until they started leaving cartons of Camels in his locker, when he was with the Cardinals." Hank knew just what I was talking about and he said he could do one better. "I was playing in this home run derby in Puerto Rico; I hit nine home runs. For every one I hit, I got a carton of cigarettes. I never smoked before baseball either. Next thing I knew, I was smoking quite a few packs a day. I'm happy to say I haven't smoked in over 40 years." (In 1960, Hank appeared in a Camel cigarette ad. He later told me that he deeply regretted being part of that ad.)

Hank went on to explain that the home run derbies were a great way of making extra money, as Major League salaries were not that great back then. It's hard to believe, but Hank's salary in his MVP year was about $40,000. In his 20 year career, he made a total about $1,500,000. Today, that's about half a year's salary for a player that can barely hit 200.

GOODBYE POP

I vividly remember the night Pop and my grandmother were driving out for my 12 birthday. We planned to go to The Watermill Inn, and they were running about two hours late. We were all starting to worry. There were no cell phones, no texting and no twitter in 1973. You just waited for people and thought the worst. If the people you were waiting for didn't show up, after a while you started calling hospitals. Really.

Finally, a mangled green Maverick pulled in the driveway like a wounded soldier. They had been in accident on the way. Pop had to skip dinner with us that night because his back was killing him. He had a cut over his eye and was very shaken up. Pop asked if he could just lie on the couch. He had to be in really bad shape not to come out for my birthday.

1973 was a tough year for a 12 year old kid who worshipped both the Mets and his grandfather. The Mets lost the World Series in seven games to the Oakland A's and Pop's doctor said the car accident apparently triggered some sort of bone cancer that we didn't know he had. On Christmas day in 1973, I lost my grandfather, my best friend and the man who was always in my corner. He was 65 years old. I couldn't believe it and didn't know how I would or could go on without him. Pop was always enthusiastic, optimistic, and hopeful. He bestowed me with those qualities. Pop always saw the good in people and always helped everyone. He had a great attitude. I know that I inherited my positive attitude from Pop.

After Pop's diagnosis, we drove to the hospital in the Bronx every weekend to see him. We would pick up chocolate covered cherries from the Lake Deli and bring them to the hospital. They were Pop's favorite It got to a point where Pop would hardly eat anything at all. He'd have one or two of his chocolate covered cherries, and tell me to have the rest. That's when I suspected things were getting worse and it hit me that Pop probably wouldn't leave the hospital. We tried to continue on with life as if everything was okay. On Christmas Eve, we kept our tradition and went to the D'Amico's house. The next morning (Christmas Day) the phone rang, and my mom wasn't saying anything. She was just listening. Then she started to cry. I was a twelve year old kid who never had anybody die on me before. I asked Mom if Pop died and she couldn't even answer, but I knew he did. My mom went upstairs to the bedroom and shut the door. I went upstairs to my bedroom shut the door, and cried. Pop was dead and there was nothing anyone could do about it. I think Pop died on Christmas Day because he was the best gift anyone could ever get. Especially me! But I guess that day they needed him for someone else.

I don't know if I realized it then, but it was the worst day of my life by a mile. When you reflect back on your life, you can be pretty accurate in determining the worst day of your life. While I haven't had that many worst days to choose from, this is the one that sticks out.

The second worst day of my life was when my beloved sheepdog, Patches, passed away during the writing of this book. I will miss him every day.

(Patches and I)

My family made all the standard funeral arrangements. At his service, I didn't want to go up to the casket, as I wanted to remember Pop alive and with a smile on his face. My mom said I should, so I did. I prayed, told him I loved him, cried, blessed myself and I'm crying now writing this. I miss you Pop, and have missed you since the day you left me. I said goodbye to Pop and promised him that throughout my life, I would make him proud.

Each year, Christmas has a special meaning for me. I miss James Angley (Pop), but I see things much differently now. The years that I got to know Pop were really a gift. If I could have a conversation with Pop right now, here's what I would share with him:

I'm not a kid anymore Pop! Remember taking me to see Tommie Agee play for the Mets? We actually became very good friends. Remember when you took me to Washington DC? Every hotel was booked and we finally found a Holiday Inn in Virginia. Well, I've been back to the White House a few times since, but as a guest of the President. I sat at the table next to JFK Jr. and Carolyn Bessette-

Kennedy! I know Pop, I can't believe it myself sometimes. My life has turned out to be quite interesting. I wish I could have returned the favor and brought you to a few places. I wish I could have looked after you the way you looked after me. Sure, all the things we did were cool, but what really resonated with me was that you taught me how to treat people. You

(*1969 New York Mets Outfield,*
Art Shamsky, Me, Tommie Agee, Ron Swoboda)

taught me to be selfless, and enjoy doing things for others. You were so right about that. You were always nice to everyone no matter who they were.

Doing something for somebody else beats doing something for yourself, every time.

I remember you always brought White Castle burgers when you came out to visit us in Long Island. It seemed that no matter how many you brought, they would disappear faster than your car could pull in the driveway. There is nothing like a sack full of White Castles - the original slider! My friends would find excuses to hang around if they knew you were coming out to visit. You always got me special ones with no onions, and put them in a separate bag. These are great memories Pop and guess what? I still love White Castle and always think of you when I go there. As a kid, you learn about relationships from your friends, parents and grandparents. You were a shining

example and I will always be grateful for the time we had together and for teaching me the value of friendship. Today, I have so many great relationships and such a great family. And I never tell my kids to rake the leaves!

It is our pleasure to invite you to
THE NEW YORK DAILY NEWS
White House Correspondents' Association Dinner
Saturday, May 1, 1999

(*My sweet White House invite*)

17

RARE GRANDMOTHER DOMINANCE

My grandfather, rest his soul, was always deathly afraid of my grandmother. My grandmother was a nurse who was paid to take in, and care for WWII military veterans. My grandparents had a five bedroom brownstone on Tremont Avenue in the Bronx. Whenever I visited them, I would

(My Grandmother)

accompany her like a young candy striper as she made the rounds to take care of her veterans. I would watch her every move as each one got her warm greeting, a variety of pills to swallow and a shot of B-12. Eventually, each of the fellows would pass away in grandma's care, and coincidentally leave my grandmother all their money. My father told me she gambled away each veteran's life savings at the horse track. I always remember when my grandmother was headed out for a night at the racetrack. She would hire a personal driver, sport a beautiful dress and fresh hairdo, and have a twinkle in her eye. There was one instance where she even offered to place a bet for me.

She said, "Stevie, give me your favorite number for the first race tonight. When you win, I'll bring you home the money, but you have to hide it from that rotten bastard father of yours." I told her that my favorite number was Tommy Agee's number, 20. She told me that I needed a lower number, because only eight or nine horses run together at the most. So I picked number three, for Bud Harrelson, because he was a real good shortstop.

I woke up the next morning and came down for breakfast. Grandma was in the kitchen as always. She told me number three had won, and I won fifty dollars. She said she only bet twenty but he was a good horse and the way the odds worked, twenty won me fifty. She said that my win in the first race gave her luck all night long. She put my fifty dollar bill in a small tan envelope, and said to hide it in my jeans pocket and then again in one of my books when I got home. She said, "Your miserable father will never look in a book, the money will be safe." In that moment I felt rich, as fifty dollars could last a kid an entire summer, or even two. I never had even close to fifty dollars before. My father said he knew why my grandmother took care of the war veterans. He claimed she would murder one of them every now and then so she could get their money faster. He said she either smothered them with a pillow, or gave them an overdose.

A few weeks later, I thought to ask my grandfather about this.

"Pop, does Grandma murder the military veterans and take their money?"

"No Stevie, the only person she wants to murder is me. If I ever get murdered, tell the police your grandmother did it, or she hired somebody to kill me. But Stevie, I am leaving your grandmother long before she gets the chance."

"Are you getting a divorce, Pop?"

"No Stevie, not a divorce. I'm just running away from her, where she will never find me!"

"Where will you go, Pop?"

"Florida."

"When?"

"Soon as I see you off to college. Maybe you will go to college in Florida. They have good baseball schools and you could play year-round. All the Mayor League teams have their spring training in Florida." My grandfather was a man with two goals: seeing me go to college, and escaping from my grandmother.

I would be the first member of my family to ever attend college. My grandmother was insane in the eyes of most people; however, I was her favorite and she looked out for me. If I spent a full day with Grandma, she said my dad was no good a hundred times. A full weekend and it was five or six hundred times. Guess what? I knew it already and didn't need her telling me. I lived with him full-time. But Grandma had her stories to back it up. A weekend at grandma's always led to an interrogation chat at some point.

"How many times did the bastard beat you this week?"

"Does he beat your brother too?"

"I've seen him beat the dog with my own two eyes! A helpless beagle!"

"He beat you this week didn't he?"

She would work herself into a froth.

"Take off your clothes."

"Why Grandma?" I asked

"You need to be checked for bruises!" I would strip down to my underwear, and stand like I was in the nurse's office. She carefully examined me from head to toe. I think she was hoping for bruises. As I dressed, she would talk about how many wonderful fellas my mother could have married. Then she would detail the travesty of how she ever allowed her to marry my father. Once she talked herself out on my father, she poured herself a cold beer and went right to work on my grandfather.

"Your grandfather is no good you know, Stevie."

"Why did you marry him Grandma?" I asked.

"I don't know. I learned he was no good afterward."

I hated to see my Grandmother torment Pop. If he was running late from work she would measure out the bleach and we would wait on the outside steps for him. I would beg Grandma not to blind him with the bleach when he came home late from work.

"You know why he is late Stevie? He is giving out taxi cab rides to his no good relatives. They are all drunken Irishmen that can't afford cars. So he sneaks them around behind my back! When he gets home he is getting bleach right between the eyes! Blind men can't drive!" Grandma said. She would then threaten to throw bleach in my father's eyes. At this, I would act sad and make believe I was crying until she would take me in the house and pour the bleach in the sink.

THEY TOOK OUR SHIP FOREVER

I remember staying with Grandma in the Bronx over winter break. She would spend the entire day in the kitchen listening to station 1010 WINS on the radio. It was snowing and grandma was making me hot chocolate and a steak sandwich for lunch. She loved to cook and I loved her rye steak sandwiches. She would lightly toast and butter the rye bread. I would ask for ketchup and she would get all upset and say "Stevie, you never put ketchup on steak", then she would give in and hand me the ketchup anyway.

Best of all she kept a smoke free house. She didn't smoke and my grandfather had to smoke outside or on the fire escape, otherwise he would get beaten with a broomstick, or threatened with the bleach. As the day wore on there was breaking news on the radio about the USS Pueblo. She was very concerned.

"Stevie, the news is saying they took our ship."

"What ship grandma?"

"The Pueblo"

'Who took it?"

"The slants!"

"What slants grandma?"

"The sneaky ones, the same slants that attacked Pearl Harbor. Pan faces!"

"What is a pan face?"

"A no good slant."

I was confused, but accepted her definition. I guess she meant Chinese or Japanese or some type of Asian person. Grandma went on to tell me about Pearl Harbor and the slants that were sneaky and no good, just like my father. I listened intently like I was hearing it all for the first time.

"Our boys were all asleep and the no good slants came during the night. It was a sneak attack. The slants have always been sneaky. They killed our young men and sunk our ships. Even the Chinaman where we get the good won ton soup, in Parkchester, he is sneaky too. Trust me."

She then realized that despite the missing ship, my grandfather wasn't home. How could the man still be at work, while they took our ship? She called Aunt Marie and Uncle George and Uncle Billy, then

Cousin Sissy and Aunt Evelyn. With each phone call she became more animated in her description of how they took the ship and were holding everyone hostage. She kept calling relatives and getting everyone all worked up, including me. She made another round of calls to the same relatives. She said all the same things, but was getting angrier with each phone call.

"If your grandfather isn't home soon he's getting bleach in his eyes!" She reached into the cabinet and measured out the bleach like a mad scientist. I was terrified. I started crying.

"Grandma, please put away the bleach."

In he walked at about 6:30 pm; he looked frail, old, freezing and dirty. I gave him a big hug and was so happy to see him.

"Pop!" I screamed.

I figured the happier I was to see him, the less likely my grandmother would hit him with the bleach. He asked my grandmother to pour him a cup of coffee.

"You sly bastard Angley, how can you ask for coffee, you know what happened today!"

"What happened, is everyone okay? Did anything happen to any of the grandkids???"

"So you going to play possum with me," said my grandmother.

At this point my grandfather was getting agitated; he just wanted his coffee.

"Today, I got up at 5:30 AM and went to the yard and got my truck. I pushed the truck all day, worked through lunch, didn't have any supper and now I just want to have coffee and talk to my Stevie."

"They took our ship today you goddamn communist."

My grandfather was obviously not in tune with the events of the day, as his truck didn't even have a radio. He told my grandmother he was turning 61 soon, maybe it wasn't too late to enlist. He said he was already fighting in two world wars - one with her every night and one with his boss every morning. He put his coat back on and he took me out to the luncheonette where we went to get coffee. I got hot chocolate. He told me at the luncheonette that my grandmother was crazy and that he should pack his stuff and get the hell out of there. He told me he needed to show me something. We left the luncheonette and he lifted up his shirt. He told me to look at his back. I saw a great big long scar. He told me that when he was younger he was stabbed, in the back. He had a fight with Irish gang members. That's why I had to go to college, so I can work with my mind, not my hands. He didn't want me working in the streets. He almost died from the stab wound. He also stabbed people and went to jail for a while.

Grandma only slightly threatened him with the bleach when we got home, but he shrugged it off as she was busy listening intently on the new developments. Grandma did not want to get far from the radio. She was pacing and carrying on about the ship. As I was getting ready for bed, she told me that I should get up early the next day and she would make me a great breakfast and together we would listen to see if we got the ship back. So the next morning I had a great breakfast. She made me grilled cheese and bacon, and hash browns ketchup, but no onions. Grandma made everything exactly how I liked it, so I told her I hoped we would get the ship back.

When my mother made hash browns they were always with onions so I didn't eat them. She said the same thing every time. "Stephen, you can't even see them." Okay, if I can't even see them, why do I have a dozen of them on the napkin next to my plate? When my father made hash browns we had to eat them, so I picked out the onions and gave them to princess under the table. He said when he was growing up they couldn't afford onions in the hash browns. In my opinion, this was still not a good enough reason to eat them.

This is not meant to be a history book, but the taking of the Pueblo was a huge international incident. I lived through it from my grandmother's kitchen radio.

THE SUMMER OF '69

In those days we had a milkman. My morning regimen included bringing in the milk and getting the newspaper from the mailbox. The milk was delivered in thick glass bottles with foil caps and I could drink half a bottle in one shot. We had this special wire rack that we would leave out on the stoop with our empties the night before and at the crack of dawn, they would magically transform to full once again. On a special occasion like a birthday, we would be treated to chocolate milk and then during Christmas season, the milkman would also deliver egg nog. Boy did I look forward to egg nog. Those were the good old days when I could see all my ribs and didn't know or care about how much I ate or drank. 1969 was a fantasy summer for Mets fans. I would take the newspaper and go outside and read it on the Indian furniture. I'd go to my usual sunny spot in the back yard to see if the Mets won and if Tommie Agee hit a home run. This was my childhood version of meditation and relaxation. Back then nothing beat just being left alone; I guess I feel the same way forty years later!

Anyway, Tommie Agee meant everything to me. So I'm eight years old in '69 and we have the perfect storm in New York Sports. The Mets win the World Series, the Jets win the Super bowl and the Knicks win the NBA Championship. I thought that was the same year the Nets won the ABA title with Dr. J and Larry Kenon. (Actually while the Nets were only one of two teams to win multiple times, their championship years were 1972 and 1974.) 1969 is also the year we even put a man on the moon (not true) and he swung a golf club. Every day people fail at the simplest tasks, yet forty years ago we sent a lunar module up to the moon. Were we smarter then, or are we just too lazy now? (I know the answer; we staged it.)

Well anyway, everyone was talking about us sending people to the moon. At night, I would go outside, look at the stars and think. Think about anything and everything. Looking up at the moon and knowing we were sending a spaceship up there was amazing to comprehend when you're eight years old. My mom was also slightly interested, as once in a while the moon stuff made the dinner table conversation.

My father was down on the whole astronauts/moon thing. He said they took too much money out of his paycheck. Half the day he drove the truck for NASA and the trip to the moon, the other half of the day he paid for Vietnam and on Saturdays he worked for the lowlifes on welfare. Every Thursday he would open the check, see how many hours of overtime he had worked and scrutinize the deductions. Then he would tell everyone "I worked nineteen hours overtime so everyone here could eat." Then he would recite the amounts of the deductions. There was no way he knew who took what, but he was certain where his tax dollars were being spent. He then threatened to get a job "off the books." That would even things up. "I'm gonna get a job off the books and everybody can kiss my ass."

That year we all watched the lunar landing on TV and it was very exciting. I was fascinated and my father said he was only watching to see what his money was paying for. Then he said he was working overtime tomorrow in case we wanted to send these assholes somewhere else in their space ship, and if they had a few bucks left, they could put another couple of lowlifes on welfare. Almost as much as welfare, he really hated tolls. Back then it was the honor system. They hadn't invented the gates yet. It was simply plastic baskets that you would throw your change into.

When we went through the toll at the Throgs Neck Bridge (over the East River) on the way to see my grandparents in the Bronx, he would scream, "Screw you Lindsay!" I believe it was Mayor Lindsay that he was upset with. Anyway, we never paid the tolls. My mother always said we would be chased by the cops and arrested, but he didn't care. He said the cops were all just eating donuts somewhere counting the days till they got their pensions, which he was paying for.

THEY WERE TWO GOODFELLAS

Twenty five years later, I'm at a golf outing for the State Trooper Foundation. I'm at the first tee, waiting to meet the others that will make up my foursome, and not looking forward to the day. Golf is not the right sport for a guy that has 46 unreturned voicemails, and long list of things to do. As I'm thinking about these things, I hear a voice from behind me. "I think you're in my foursome." I turn around and he says, "I'm Tommie Agee." My heart pounds and my knees weaken. I gather myself up, catch my breath and introduce myself. "I'm Stephen Costello, from P.C. Richard and Son." "I've heard that name before," said Tommie. "Do you deal with a lot of the former players? I think Art Shamsky and Ron Swoboda have mentioned your name before."

Tommie Agee learned that day that he was my favorite player growing up, because I told him 453 times. And I really meant it. I spent that day stalking, more than golfing. But wait, it gets better! After Tommie introduced himself, I found out that Tony Darrow was in our foursome as well. Tony Darrow played Sonny Bunz in my favorite movie of all time, Goodfellas. (Tommy hits Sonny over the head with a bottle at Bamboo Lounge.)

I told Tony that Goodfellas was my favorite movie, and that I had seen it more times than my grandmother said my father was no good. And my grandmother lived to 94. So I'm stalking two guys at once. All while golfing and returning my messages between holes. Quite a day at the golf course! Tommie and I grew to be very close friends; he was as good a guy as a player. We would plan family dinners, usually at Vincent's in Carle Place, NY. (*Author's note: Vincent's Clam Bar is my favorite place in the world to eat dinner with friends and family.*)

Tommie became one of the guys in my corner. At the end of this of this book, I'm putting together my 'people in my corner' list, and he's on it. The day Tommie passed away

(*Me with my favorite player ever, Tommie Agee.*)

in 2001 was a rough day. It happened out of nowhere; he had a heart attack while walking out of his office at Titleserv. Tommie will always be known for making two of the greatest catches in World Series history, and he did them in the same game in 1969. To this day, I play in his memorial golf outing and it always brings me back to the day we met. You bet that Tommie goes on my 'in my corner' list. He was my childhood hero who became a great friend.

In my office there is a cherished picture of Tommie with the words, 'To my friend Stephen' written on it. Hanging on the celebrity photo wall at Vincent's Clam Bar is also a picture of me and Tommie. There we are, smack in the middle. It's the place we generally met for lunch. (If you see it, you'll note that my last name is misspelled, 'Castello' but I'm just thankful to have my picture up there with Tommie so I leave it alone.)

Tony Darrow is another story. He and I clicked instantly, like brothers. It's a weird phenomenon when you meet someone and the next thing you know they're on your speed dial, like you've known them forever. That's the two of us. We go to cigar parties and fundraisers together, and I always bring him in as the comedian and MC for my own golf outings. In turn, he has offered me a few extra roles in his movies, but I can never fit them in my schedule! He runs an annual golf outing and has raised over a million dollars for Cerebral Palsy research. Interestingly, Tony got the role in *Goodfellas* due to Martin Scorsese seeing him in a very small role in the 1987 horror/comedy movie, *Street Trash*.

Later in his career, Tony was in several more movies including *Analyze This*, and also appeared in many episodes of the hit HBO series, *The Sopranos*. We both agree that everything you need to know about life is in the movie *Goodfellas*. It's similar to the epic movie

(A thank you from Tony Darrow with the rest of The Goodfellas - Ray Liotta, Joe Pesci, Robert DeNiro, and Martin Scorsese)

The Godfather. Being Italian and growing up in the Bronx, well, these movies hit close to home. My dad was in the Teamsters. There were always whispers and questions about who he knew that was mobbed up. Anyway, try this...stand in the middle of a big crowd and say, "Karen came to the house." At least half will know what you're talking about and the other half, who cares? Here's another one: "I only use them for certain things." People are and always have been obsessed with the mob, plain and simple. Just look at the popularity of *The Sopranos*. When I look back to that incredible golf outing where I met Tommie and Tony, it's surreal that of all the foursomes that day, I wound up with my favorite baseball player, and an actor from my favorite movie. There was something special about that day, and it's not something I could put my finger on but for some reason, these two guys are voluntarily part of my everyday life. Perhaps they saw those traits in me that I inherited from Pop.

Networking and relationship building is not important, it is everything. It's a game changer and a life changer.

They don't have bachelor's degrees in networking or developing relationships. I was told by my good friend, Peter Shankman, that I run into a cocktail party like a fireman runs into a burning building. He's another guy in my corner. Peter is brilliant, polite, brilliant one more time, lovable, authentic, famous, and my friend. One day I took my daughter, Madison, to Barnes and Noble in Boston. I bought Peter's most recent book, *Nice Companies Finish First*. I read the book cover to cover on the ride home. I loved it. I knew that day

(My Wake Up Call! Madison and I buying Peter's book, "Nice Companys Finish First." I bought the book and was committed to writing my own)

I would be an author, no question about it. Peter has been my dugout manager like Don Zimmer was to Joe Torre. I have learned much from

Peter, but the greatest thing he ever said to me was this: "Take the 'sorrys' out of the book! You don't have to be sorry about anything. Your life is your life; your book is your book. Never forget that." When I got home that night I deleted all the apologies. If you're not familiar with him already, I'm glad to introduce you to Peter Shankman. He generously offered to pen a few thoughts for this book:

"Hi there, everyone. I'm interjecting in the middle of Steve's book because he asked me to, and Steve is one of those people who could ask me to swim the English Channel, and I'd book the next flight to Heathrow. You don't meet many people like that. After spending the day with Steve at the 2013 Baseball All Star Game, I wrote the following (below) for my business blog at www.shankman.com. Watching Steve at that event was a thing of beauty. He spent the entire game talking to everyone, but not just talking...listening. Listening, and asking how he could help. THAT'S the definition of awesome networking. I hope this post helps you. If you have any thoughts on it, shoot me an email - Peter@Shankman. com - I'm always up for feedback."

"I was fortunate enough to be invited to the 2013 Baseball All Star Game last night, by the wonderful people at Steiner Sports. In between shoveling hot dogs, pasta, and fresh sliced steak into my mouth, I talked to a lot of people. I also watched the person who invited me [Stephen Costello] - He's a master networker. Between the two of us, I offer you five networking takeaways that I both learned and employed at Citi Field last night, and that are applicable anywhere.

5) Get a beer for anyone. I've been doing this for years, and it paid off last night - The tables in the lounge I was in at the game (Thank you, Modells!) were all high-bar tables, meaning you'd meet new people whenever you sat down, as there was no assigned seating. Easiest thing in the world - If I was getting back up to stuff my face, I'd simply bring back another round of whatever everyone else was drinking. Granted, this is easier at an open bar. But come on, who doesn't like the guy who shows up with another round for everyone? Got three business cards and one "Oh, your new company sounds interesting - Call me," out of three beers and a vodka soda.

4) Recommend food. It was a buffet line, with chefs behind the pasta bar, the meat bar, and the hot dog bar. (Yes, Modell's clubhouse at Citi Field had a hot dog bar.) I had my first plate of pasta when I walked in the door. By the time I went up for a second one, the woman in front of me was having a hard time choosing. I simply told her what I had, and that it was awesome. We then had four minutes to schmooze while the pasta was being prepared. Another intro. And when I email her today to tell her it was nice to meet her and offer a little more about what I do, I can simply title the email "From Pasta Guy." Everyone loves Pasta Guy. Or Steak Guy. Or Burger Guy.

3) Be the guy who takes the photo. I spent last night in the company of giants. Literally. Darryl Strawberry. Steve Schirripa, Mitchel Modell. As I wandered the clubhouse, I saw more and more people attempting bad selfies with celebrities. A selfie with a celebrity is never a good idea because a) you'll always look awkward at best, and b) you'll more than likely have six chins from holding your head back to try and get in the shot. Selfies are bad in general, super-bad with a celeb. So I would walk around, and when I saw someone try and take the photo, I'd offer to take their camera and take the picture for them. The sense of relief that came over the person was massive. They could look their best for a photo that you know damn well was going to be on their Facebook page two seconds later. Bonus? I could talk to them, and if I wanted to talk more, ask them to friend me so I could see the photo.

2) Find someone else who's as awestruck by how their life rolls as you are. As I walked outside of the clubhouse and into the "outside" part of the clubhouse, which was essentially, the warning track in center field, I stopped for a second and offered a small prayer of thanks. Come on - I'm nobody special. I'm not an actor on TV; I'm not a baseball player or a sports star. I'm a guy who got lucky with a few companies, and who tries to live by a code of being good to people. That's gotten me almost everything in my life I have - My wife, my child, my cat, my success - But when I stand next to Cy Young Award Winners, or Tony/Oscar winners... I'm just floored. I'm like, "dude, I'm just a kid who grew up in the NYC public schools - What the heck am I doing here?" It's an amazing feeling, and if you look hard enough, you'll find someone else with that same kind of "holy crap, this is ridiculous!" grin on their face. Friend them. You'll have a connection for life based on something no one can take away. Some of the people I do the most business with are also NYC kids, just as amazed at where their life is taking them as I am with mine.

1) Finally, you're in a small space - Just turn to the person next to you and start talking! At the very least, do this. You're at an event. It's a fun event. People are having a good time. There's no reason not to talk to someone who's having just as good a time as you, at the same event! You don't even have to make it about work if you don't want to. In fact, it's always good to start off NOT about work - Work will always be there. Start off with something fun. Last night, it was hot as anything when we walked out of the clubhouse. Something as simple as "I wonder if they'll bring over the hoses they use to wet down the infield dirt over here?" was a nice opener. Just talk to people. You'll be amazed what comes of it."

Networking is life. Never forget that.
Good Networking = Good Life.

Best,
Peter Shankman

MY FRIENDS?

So I pushed ahead on my goal of getting old enough to move out of my house and participated in the crazy relationship with my three best friends, Peter, Jimmy, and Mark. The better we knew each other and the older we got, the worse the rank-out sessions were. When you look back, you realize that your relationships with your adolescent friends really shape you. I wonder if this was a good thing, or bad thing. Anyway, my friends were well on the road to growing up to be detectives. Anything you did, said, or wore, got you called out immediately. Think about it, these were supposed to be my friends— they were rough. If your pants were just slightly too short they yelled "flood!" If your shirt was too big it was your father's. Too small, it was your mother's and if you had a pocket on your shirt, it was your grandfather's. If it was plaid it was a table cloth. This all could happen within one outfit. They were brutal, really brutal.

The school changed my bus stop in fifth grade, so I had to walk a quarter of a mile past Peter's house and over near the park. It was after my birthday, September 29th, and it was starting to get colder. My grandmother got me a great Mets jacket, and my friends were immediately jealous of it. I endured at least three days of insults about my grandmother…the coat…why couldn't she have bought in my size…on and on. I'm shocked I still even remember this agonizing banter. Anyway, the following Monday my friends have this contest all cooked up. Which of us can go the longest to the bus stop without wearing a coat? They knew I hated the cold, but I was also extremely competitive. Let the contest begin, and let's start freezing to death. I had to walk down the windy hill of Radburn Drive, the Bill Groll danger zone, and had the furthest distance to the bus stop. It was near Thanksgiving and it had already snowed twice. Each morning I would take a good long look at my scarf, gloves, and very warm snorkel coat. Most people reading this probably don't even know what a snorkel coat is. It was green, with a hood that had fake fur around it. Who the hell knows, maybe it was real fur back then. Everyone had one, because we all had the same things. They were very warm.

My mother didn't understand what was at stake. Every morning, she said I would get pneumonia and have to go see Dr. Fried, and then to the hospital. "Please, put a jacket on! You're crazy! If your friends all jumped off a bridge would you jump too?" Hmmmm…great question. So out I went into the cold, Monday thru Friday. Finally, one morning it occurred to me. What the hell am I doing? Why am I freezing my ass off every day? I learned the best lesson of my life that day. Who cares what people think, especially those idiots? I took out the scarf, the Snorkel, my warm as toast gloves and slipped into all with a victorious smile on my face. If hand warmers were invented back then, I would have grabbed those, too. I convinced myself I won the contest. The loser was the winner. Off I went to the bus stop and watched these three idiots freezing to death. Sure, I got called Mary Jane, Emily and other girl's names. But I was warm. I didn't care! The next morning, needless to say, everyone wore coats. The contest was over. I looked at it this way: winning was being the first to wear a coat, not the last. I changed the rules; I mentally manipulated them.

Be yourself, and be true to yourself. Stop caring about what other people think.

I learned this lesson 40 years ago but heard it again recently at a trip to Coach Knight's house. He told me the day he became a great coach is the day he stopped thinking about what people thought. Guess I knew that already.

(One of my many trips to see Coach Knight.)

I MADE THE BASKETBALL TEAM

Athletics were really the driving force of our childhood and we played everything. Baseball, football, stickball, tennis, bowling…you name it. Once you reach Junior High and start competing and trying out for the school team, you really see what level everyone is at, for real. For so many years we all thought that we were the same, but we knew Jimmy was the fastest and I could throw the farthest. We also predicted who win in a fight, but thankfully, it never got to that. We just had your run-of-the-mill skirmishes. Then we would rank each other. In baseball, I was the best. In basketball and football I thought I was the best, but the other three ranked me as the worst. So it was a real shining moment when I made the basketball team at Sagamore Junior High School and my three best friends got cut. Shove your rankings up your ass! We ain't in Kansas anymore, boys. My three best friends were cut. What a shame. Trust me, it was special. We were not all the same anymore. I was finally better at something! That day was a game changer for me. It was like getting a 50 lb. bag of confidence delivered to your house.

When they wanted to make plans after school, I had to let them know I had basketball practice. Those words came so sweetly off of my tongue. Mark, who proclaimed he was the best of us in hoop, actually sent his mother to see the coach and beg for his place on the team. No dice! She even brought his YMCA trophies! I swear it's true!

Let's just say in the early years I struggled with girls. To be fair, I really struggled. My first crush was Missy Morin. Actually, it was probably my sixth crush overall, but the first five had absolutely no interest in me, and stalking wasn't invented yet. So you licked your wounds and tried for the next girl you liked. Anyway, Missy liked me. Yeah! I probably liked Missy too much. So we did the make-believe dating thing, the leather ID bracelets and all of that. Missy and I were going steady…that's what they called it!

(*Braces, NBA Ball, and a Dr. J Poster*)

So, for about two months we were going steady, and then I got braces. I wasn't certain about the kissing thing. I felt weird kissing her with braces on. She felt weird too, because we had a common friend, Kim, who would tell me what Missy thought, and would tell Missy what I thought. We ran the entire relationship through Kim. Finally, she told me Missy wasn't interested in going steady anymore, but she (Kim) really liked me a lot. She was six inches taller than me with a slightly crooked face. No dice. I lost them both, only to find out later on that Missy still liked me but by then it was too late. Pete was seeing a girl named Dawn who was so, so hot. She probably is still now. Mark, on the other hand, was asking out every girl and kept getting turned down. We were actually eyewitnesses to a girl telling Mark "no" when he asked her out in the hall at Sagamore. We made a joke out of it for the next five or six years, or maybe it was more like ten, or twenty years? One of us would play Mark, and the other would pretend to be the girl:

"Hi, do you want to go to the movies with me?"

"NO!"

Then we would all crack up. It was brutal! When I came home from college and met up with them, we would start it all over again and crack up like teenagers.

I knew I was making the baseball team, but I was nervous about my chances in football. I could catch anything, but junior high football sucked for me. We had this guy, Al Doll, who got held back three times. At least! As you can imagine, he was bigger than the rest of the team. We would run fifty end sweeps, always giving the ball to Al Doll, and he would run over the other team like a steamroller. That's how we won. It was the high school version of the Lombardi Packers.

I got to watch, freeze, or block. I still remember pushups in the freezing cold; jumping jacks in the freezing cold; hitting your freezing body against the freezing sled; then hitting each other. People actually stayed after school for this kind of punishment!

I could throw the ball a mile but nobody seemed to care. Why are all the guys that got held back the stars of the team? Because they are two and three years older than the average kid. If I had it to do all over again, I would look at it a bit differently. I liked football; I just didn't love it then. I grew to love it later. Anyway, all four of us made the football team: Peter was the quarterback (even though I could throw further), Mark and Jimmy were linebackers and I switched between wide receiver and linebacker. I was wide receiver on a team that had not yet heard about the forward pass - and when they did, it wasn't to me - so most of my time was spent attempting to block larger, older kids that got held back. If they would have studied more, all the players would have been my age, in which case I probably could have blocked them. I was always on the losing end of the steamroller.

My mom would come to the football games with as many people as she could get – relatives and her neighborhood friends. Because the helmets all looked alike, and offense and defense kept getting swapped out, nobody ever knew how much I actually played, or didn't. Perfect. Watching football can be really confusing. In actuality, I probably played more playing time than I deserved. The relatives would all say how well I played, but football was frustrating. On the school team, I just couldn't find my rhythm. You learn about humility when you can't control all the variables. You can't make the coach have passes thrown to you. You can't redesign the team's game plan. I just decided I would keep working hard. I was playing enough and I was on the team. So I just started working much harder. I wanted to belong and I wanted to succeed.

Friday was awesome. The games were on Saturday so we were allowed to wear our jerseys and jeans in school. Everyone knew you were on the football team. This was important to me. I wore my jersey proudly. We won most of the time, except against Wyandanch, Brentwood, or Amityville. I think everyone on those teams were held back a few years; they would just kill us. I remember a few of those guys had mustaches and chin hairs. I'd study my face closely, and didn't see a single hair while these guys were breaking out beards and goatees.

LET'S GET A BOAT!

I'm sure you have all seen those pharmaceutical commercials where the father and son go fishing together. They smile and laugh, and then it gets serious while the dad tells his son about his high cholesterol, but then it's happy horseshit again. Things didn't go that way for me.

Our first boat was an eighteen foot Wizard, I believe, with an aluminum trailer. My dad proudly proclaimed himself the Captain. Those types of boats were too small to have a captain but you couldn't tell my father that. So, the Wizard boat sat in the driveway, on dry dock. My Dad brought home a few odds and ends for it. One night he brought home life preservers. Another night he brought home a depth finder. Anything he brought home would be accompanied by an announcement, as if we didn't know what it was.

"See these here, PRESERVERS!"

I had already processed that they were preservers, and figured I would be wearing one before long. A fishing trip was on the horizon, as my father brought home lures and poles, albeit nicer that the bamboo poles we would hang off the dock with to catch snappers. A big Friday night for the Costello family was getting take-out from Flo's. I liked Flo's, and the prices were cheap, so my father would allow us to order whatever we wanted. I would get a Milkshake, cheeseburger and onion rings. We would look at all the boats in Corey Creek, and wonder out loud how anyone had enough money to buy them. After our meal at Flo's, the family would walk along the dock and look for unsuspecting crabs. We always brought a flashlight, a net and a small cooler. My job was to shine the flashlight. My father would capture them in the net. The dock was a stupid place to be for a crab, but nonetheless, every time we went we took home a dozen or so. The ride home was always the same conversation. My father imagined how much the crabs would be at 'that place' in Centereach. He would ask us the name of the place, but I would just say I didn't know, even though I did. It was Centereach Fish Market. It was the fish market in Centereach for God's sake. Not that difficult. The conversation turned to how much money my father saved the family by catching them instead of buying them. It started with twenty dollars, then thirty dollars and by the time we got home, we had over fifty dollars' worth of crabs.

When we arrived home, he would fill the cooler with ice, and put a rock on the cover. He didn't want to lose our treasure to a hungry raccoon. Then he would go outside and check on the crabs before he went to bed. The following day, my mother would have to make crab-something. Crab salad, crab cakes, spaghetti with crab sauce…there was never a shortage of what you could do with a dozen free crabs. I didn't like

(Best place for a boat, on land)

crab meat, so I always passed. As the rest of the family ate the various crab dishes my father boasted how they tasted better because we caught them fresh. He would question the quality of the crabs at the fish market.

"They probably get 'em cheap from the japs, freeze 'em, then they rob us. "

"Dad, the crabs at the fish market are alive, so I doubt they get 'em from the Japs. And I doubt they freeze them."

He told me for a guy who didn't eat crabs; I had a lot of fucking opinions on the subject. To this day, no form of crab has ever entered my mouth. Nor will it ever. On Sundays we would always have pasta of some sort and generally we would invite friends or relatives over. Sunday has always been my favorite day. Always will be! My mother would talk in her "Aunt Helen voice" when we had people over. She still does it to this day, trying to outdo someone. We just bought new this, and new that. The Indians brought over this beautiful outdoor furniture, and on and on. Each sentence involved more and more of an exaggeration. At least on Sunday, I got pasta and a great marinara sauce, and sometimes chicken cutlets, or sausage or meatballs.

If my grandmother was visiting for the weekend the food would be even be better, as she brought everything out from the Bronx. Everything would come right from Arthur Avenue. It was a meal right out of the Godfather. I would try to convince Grandma that her meatballs were great without the onions and garlic chunks. She would say, "Stevie, you have to have onions and garlic chunks in the meatballs." I'd make a sad face until my grandmother would say, "Okay this time I'll make the meatballs without onions and garlic. Keep it between us."

I hated onions and garlic chunks in the meatballs, so when grandma made them without, it was awesome. On Sundays in the fall I would play tackle football with my friends, and then watch the Jets and Giants on TV. I always played quarterback because I could throw the farthest. My friends would crush me, long after I threw the ball. There were no roughing the quarterback penalties back then, just my friends laughing after I complained they were trying to kill me.

Our football games were at 10 am, followed by a 'big sammie' at Lake Deli, and then back to my house to watch the games in the converted garage. A big sammie was my standard sandwich order of thinly sliced Boar's Head ham, ham cappy, genoa salami, provolone cheese, shredded lettuce and vinegar and oil. I want one NOW. I loved the smell of the sandwich in the car. Smelling it was just as awesome as eating it. One particular Saturday evening, I had a feeling that my Sunday ritual was in jeopardy. My father was preparing all kinds of fishing gear. It looked like he was preparing to bring home a great white shark. I knew fishing was generally an early morning thing; dad said that's when fish were hungry.

"Seriously, Dad, I have football tomorrow. I'm the quarterback. I can't go fishing." Then I caught myself from continuing, knowing the half hour speech I'd get about how he broke his ass to keep a roof over our heads and all that went with it. So, fishing it was...

I remember the boat and trailer was purchased for $1,100. I remember dad coming home and boasting and gloating how he robbed this hooknose wiseguy. The boat seller was no match for his advanced negotiating skills. He repeated these stories hundreds of times. The only story he kept on the down low was the inchworm story when he was lying on the ground with the two guys biting and kicking him, and that was my favorite story by far. Dad said the boat was worth almost $2500, according to a boating magazine he purchased. After carefully scrutinizing the magazine, the boat in the picture was the Queen Mary next to what he bought. I wasn't going to burst his bubble; that may have led to a beating.

I felt my role evolving from back yard rake master, to deckhand. I knew that the 'Captain' had plans for me other than trying my first beer, having a big sammie, and catching a fish. Five o'clock in the morning came quickly. It was barely light out when he poked in my room, "Steve, you up!" While he was in the only shower in the house, I had a few minutes to count the days until I left for college, and a few last minutes to lie in my bed before getting up, grabbing a glass of OJ, and accepting my fate.

He hooked up the boat and trailer to his green Chevy Blazer while I thought of all I would miss that day, knowing I would be vilified on Monday. We set for the high seas in Port Jefferson, which is on the north shore of Long Island. While my father prepared for launch, I got to hold the boat on a rope. Into the water went the boat, and he pulled away to park the Blazer.

He came back with a Chinese takeout food container, and a bag of sandwiches. As we were heading out to sea, I made sure I had on my preserver. The boat didn't seem that seaworthy to me. Then, Dad broke out the Chinese take-out container, which held seaweed and long red wormy things with a million little legs. While penning this book, I looked them up and found out their official name is Sandworms. I will never forget what they looked like. They were disgusting to look at, and disgusting to smell. He showed me how to bait a hook, which contaminated my hands with worm goo. I remember leaning over the boat to wash the warm remnants with the salt water. Before I know it, I am now driving the boat, so he can catch the fish. At 14, never drove anything before, but now I'm driving the

boat and I'm terrified. Wouldn't the captain want to drive? Nope. The boat was way too small for the body of water we were in, this I knew immediately. I was upset from the bait juice and goo, and missing football, but the real fear was no longer seeing land in any direction.

(Sandworms!)

I drove the boat slowly while he fished for mackerel. He caught a bunch, then he drove and I caught a few. The tiny boat was filled with fish – free fish! He seemed very happy and let his guard down just a bit. I think he was able to see for a moment that life is more than just being just a miserable bastard all the time. Then, like a change in the tide, another boat witnessed us catching lots of fish. I didn't know anything about fishing etiquette, but the next thing I know, my father is cursing at them and telling them to get the fuck away from our boat. They say some stuff back and now it's a shouting match filled with obscenities between my father and three decent size guys. They head straight for us, and now I'm really scared. My dad tells me to grab the sinkers. A sinker is a metal weight that holds the bait on the bottom of the sea. I barely knew what one was. The first sinker he throws, and hits the boat coming towards us.

I wind up throwing a sinker too, and it whizzes right past one of their heads. Then my father takes out the flare gun, and points it at the boat. Adrenaline is taking over and I'm getting into it. I throw one more sinker really hard, and suddenly, they turn away. They must have thought we were crazy people. All I could think was how did fishing turn into Pirates of the Caribbean? Right or wrong, I guess I learned a bit about survival that day. When it's three large men against one adult and a 14 year old kid, open up the tackle box and start firing off the sinkers.

We wrapped up the trip after that, once we couldn't see the other boat anymore. We somehow found our way back to the dock, and headed home. I figure that in a short while I'll take a shower and watch Joe Namath throw for 400 hundred yards against the Rams. But life doesn't always work that way. I got the job of filleting the mackerel and scrubbing down the boat. Filleting the mackerel was a fate worse than death. The mackerel were staring at me and there was more blood then an operating room. I was traumatized and close to passing out. I have never eaten fish to this day, and never will. Scrubbing the boat to my father's standards easily qualified me for my own boat detailing business. My father inspected the boat like it was on its way to the boat show. Hours later, I was ready to wash away the wormy stuff, the blood, the salt and the day's memories. About five minutes into the beautiful shower, he was banging on the door yelling at me not to use all the hot water. I only saw the last few minutes of the Jets' game. My mom had the sauce going, with cheese ravioli, which was my favorite. I made a plate and went to the den. Thinking about how my most favorite day of the week was lost at sea and spent filleting mackerel and cleaning the boat made my blood boil. If someone had told me to eat a plate of mackerel, I would have run away to Iowa. In bed that night I was filled with deep thought. I really couldn't stand my father. I would never own a boat. I will never eat a fish. I loved playing football. I loved watching football.

Thankfully, Monday on the bus wasn't all that bad. My friends got crushed by the team from Centereach and by the fourth stop, Jimmy admitted they needed me at quarterback. They all knew how my dad was, and I explained I couldn't get out of fishing. I told them about the three guys on the other boat and the sinkers, and soon we were all cracking up. The three of them actually wished they went fishing instead of football, so they could have thrown sinkers at the guys too, and threaten them with the flare gun.

AMERICA'S PASTIME

It was getting late in the fall, and I remember fishing only two more times. Once was at night looking for stripers. We didn't find any, thank God. No filleting and no scrubbing blood out of the boat. Soon after, my father announced he was winterizing the boat. Hooray. So out he went with a jug of anti-freeze. I could finally take a deep breath, since the fishing season was now over and the backyard was free of leaves, (and pine needles). It was clear sailing. Hold on…I almost forgot the acorns.

School baseball tryouts came next. Peter and I made the team but Jimmy and Mark got cut. Every boy in school tried out for the team. Every Friday for three weeks 'the list' was put up and everyone would sprint down the hallway to see if they made the team. The day the cut list came out, no one paid attention in class or slept the night before. This was as nerve racking as it gets. It led to cold sweats and nightmares. Everyone knew my reputation in Little League and on the travel team. I was lights out from nine to thirteen, and made the all-star team every year. In junior high, the kids trying out were really good. Eight elementary schools fed into our junior high and I was up against a lot of kids I had never seen before. The night before the list came out, I tossed and turned. My entire life hinged on my name being on that list. So I lay awake, thinking half the night about making the team, and the other half of the night about not making the team. It's absolute agony, and the only certainty is that I needed to be on that list. So I prayed about it, and on the final Friday, Mr. Dragonette posted the list. I see 'Costello'! Whewwwww!

Seeing my name on that list is something I will never forget. I remember the wall that the list hung on, like it was yesterday. I even remember the shade of blue ink Coach Dragonette wrote my name in!

Life will give you the great days; life gave me that one. Thanks!

In little league, when I wasn't pitching, I played first base. But now they had a really good first basemen, Rob Breidenbach. So now what? I pitched opening day and we won, so all was right in the world. I also got three hits. The next game I was benched because I wasn't pitching. My mother rounded up friends and family to come see me play. The games were right after school, so only my mom and her group came. My dad wasn't there as he was still at work keeping the NASA program running, and the lowlifes on welfare.

"Why didn't you play?"

"We thought you were really good."

"I'm a pitcher; pitchers don't play every game. They play when they pitch."

My mother would jump in and repeat herself, "In the Summer League you played first base when you weren't pitching. In the Summer League you played first base when you weren't pitching. In the Summer League you played first base when you weren't pitching. Can't you talk to the coach? Can't you talk to the coach? Did you tell him you're a good hitter, too? Did you tell him you're a good hitter, too?" "MOM HE SEES ME HIT EVERY DAY IN PRACTICE! HE KNOWS HOW I HIT!"

"Everybody came to see you play and everybody's upset that you're not playing."

(Where is it stated in the parenting manual that you should make your kid feel worse when he is benched?)

"Really, mom?"

The way it shook out, Briedenbach was the first baseman and it didn't seem like I could do much about it. We lost two close games and now Peter was pitching against Seneca, a rival in our district. Peter asked Coach Dragonette if I could play right field. Peter said they needed my bat in the lineup. I never knew this until years later. It was important, because we only played the other two junior high teams in the district once and those games were huge. The winner won bragging rights.

In that next game I hit for three doubles, threw out a runner at the plate and a runner at third. Peter pitched a shutout and we were off to Friendly's for patty melts and fribbles. That's one place that hasn't changed, thank goodness…Friendly's. I could still go for a fribble and a patty melt, right now. That summer wasn't so bad. My father was working a lot, although his employer, Hills Supermarkets, closed. Now he was shaping. Shaping is when you call for work at a long list of places and they call back if they need you. If you work a certain amount of days for one place they are required to hire you. It's union stuff: Teamsters, Jimmy Hoffa, rules and regulations. At the shaping places he worked midnight to eight in the morning, and then he would sleep all day. Let's call those the glory days. Then, I caught another huge break. He had an accident at work and broke his leg in nine places. His huge cast would really crimp the fishing this summer.

I looked forward to the summer travel league, as almost every team wanted me. The majority of the junior high kids played in the school travel league, but I played for my church. St. Margaret's always had the best travel teams. I knew that if I played in that league, I would bat third, pitch 'til my arm fell off and play anywhere I wanted when I wasn't pitching. My mother could bring a bus load of relatives. While the season was going on, the four of us kept up our whiffle ball tournament. That was the same time as the Watergate hearings, which fascinated me. Some days I would even get my mother to tell my friends that I wasn't home, just so I could stay tuned in to the coverage all day. They would knock on the door.

"Where's Stephen?"

"He went to play with his friends."

"No he didn't, we're his friends."

"No, he has some other friends."

"No he doesn't."

"Yes he does."

"Who?"

"I don't know their names."

"He's probably home." (Peter)

"I bet he's hiding." (Mark)

"I bet he's watching the Watergate stuff like a fag." (Jimmy)

"Yeah he's a fag" (all three in harmony).

They'd walk around the outside of the house and try to look in all the windows, to spot me. We only had one television; it was in the converted garage. It had two windows and blinds. I would lower the blinds, and they would try to see me through the crack in the bottom of the blinds. When I'd hear them that close, I'd hide in the laundry room until I thought they were gone. If they saw me, they would then ask my mother to come in the house, then torture me until I went out and played whiffle ball. Anyway, I was riveted by Watergate - my first glimpse at the corrupt nature of politics. The scary thing was that I really understood it. Well, I take that back. What I understood was the enormity of it. I realized while it was going on that this was an insane time in history and our President was on the ropes. I also realized that stuff like this probably happened all the time, but nobody ever heard about it. Two young Washington Post reporters, Woodward and Bernstein, changed history by mounting a relentless pursuit of the facts in the case. Every day that I watched, it became more interesting. That whole era came alive again in 2005 when we found out that 'Deep Throat' was former FBI agent, Mark Felt. Back in the day it was assumed that he was, but nobody knew for certain in the '70's. The identity of Deep Throat was quite possibly one of the only things my father was right about. He accused everyone and their mother of being corrupt, long before corruption was that popular.

My father was a racist in every way.

He was as racist as Archie Bunker without TV restrictions. He freely attacked all creeds, colors and religions. Our dinner table was his bully pulpit. He was so proud of his bigoted views. Back then and even more so today, I found it so disgraceful. Politicians were hooknoses and mutts. His degrading adjectives were endless. He really mastered the English language. Why is this man a truck driver and not an English teacher?

GATORADE AND THE RECAP

The St. Margaret's Cougars kicked everyone's asses that summer. I pitched a gem against Middle Island to get us to the championship game, and Mike Lopez pitched us past Terryville Port Jeff. I played centerfield as we won that game at Morris Park under the lights. Nothing beat Morris Park under the lights. It was one of the nicest fields on Long Island and you felt like you were playing in the big leagues. Huge lights, real fences and real dugouts. Morris Park was special. It was amazing! As I remember, we had Champagne and shaving cream to help celebrate our championship. I guess the adults drank the Champagne. My mother is over right now and doesn't remember the Champagne. She said we poured Gatorade on each other's heads, and crazily sprayed shaving cream everywhere. Gatorade only came in powdered packets back then. You mixed it with water and put in a big Gatorade jug. Every now and then I kick back and think of my best days. That championship was one of them. Our coach, Mr. Pecorino was another guy in my corner. He truly believed I could do anything on the baseball field. He was a short Italian guy with a deep raspy voice who threw big team parties at his house after we won a championship. He always had trays of baked ziti, extra sauce, meatballs and antipasto. My friends were jealous that they didn't play for Mr. Pecorino and they never made the finals. They would call my house and prank me with their weak impersonations of him. My Mom would scream, "it's Mr. Pecorino." When I got on the phone, one of my friends would do a poor imitation of his raspy voice and hang up. The next day we would all laugh about it.

Let's Recap. (People that know me know that I love to recap things.) I am over the 100 page mark in writing this book and if you're still with me, you haven't tossed the book out yet. So here you go…a recap.

I hope by now, this book as made you laugh once or twice. I also hope by now you've thought about people that are 'in your corner' throughout your life. I hope you've warmed up to my grandmother (kind of), and I'm sure you're glad you didn't know my father. If,

(I grew up with Gatorade when it was only a powder)

while reading this you thought for a moment about throwing bleach in somebody's eyes, DON'T DO IT! I know it's tempting. You know that I think it's a hoax that we put a man on the moon when I was eight years old, and he hit a golf ball. Harvey Haddix had the greatest game ever pitched since 1871 and Hank Aaron told me he remembers that game "oh so well" right after I knocked his coat on the floor. I love fishing. If Harvey grew up in my house, he might still be alive. He would have never smoked a cigarette in his life, just like me. If he survived the second hand smoke in my house, like I did, he never would have touched one as an adult. The only thing I haven't recapped is Harvey's game yet. I know! I'm setting the table.

I'm not going inning by inning, batter by batter, because that is not the most important thing here. But people want Sports Center, right? So I will give you an accurate, Sports Center-type account of the game, eventually. I'm fascinated by the characters that played in the game, each one worthy of a book all by themselves. There's so much I didn't know about the power of the tobacco companies, and the misinformation they give you. Corporate propaganda can be every bit as powerful as parental propaganda. Government propaganda is exactly the same. People believe something just because a person in a position of authority says it. Decades ago, Doctors were simply shills in white coats for the tobacco companies. Yes, Hank, smoking will prevent colds and sore throats. Go out and kill yourself.

So Harvey glides through 36 batters and we all know how hard that is, since it had never happened before, and hasn't happened since then. EVER. So who screwed up that perfect game? Here it is. Don Hoak, the Pirates third baseman screwed up the whole thing. Felix Mantilla hit a room service ball to Hoak at third base. Hoak took a little too much time to get that ball to Rocky Nelson at first base and just like that, Harvey's streak had come to an end. Hank, Adcock, Matthews, and all the Braves sluggers couldn't touch Harvey, but the perfect game abruptly ended on a ground ball that should have easily been an out. It might have been the easiest play of the night but instead, it was the one that ruined history. But isn't it still historic if 36 batters up and 36 batter down has never been done before? So who is Don Hoak? Let's get to know him a little bit here. A few years after the

Haddix game, he met and fell in love with the famous singer, Jill Corey. They later married. I found out he is the toughest, most loyal, standup guys in the world and was one of Harvey's best friends on the team. He's the last guy in the world you would expect to have an errant throw at the most crucial time. Sometimes your friends let you down. Ain't that the truth? Good ol' Don threw the ball low and off the bag. His throw was outrun by a speeding Felix Mantilla.

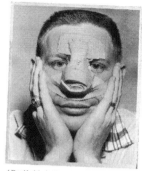

(Don Hoak broke his nose six-times, this photo was taken after his most recent surgery to repair his nose)

Don Hoak is one of only a few players in the post-World War II era to have a rule change instituted based solely on a play he made. In April 1957, Hoak was the runner on second base with Gus Bell on first and Wally Post at the plate. Post hit a groundball to the shortstop, Johnny Logan, for a seemingly sure double-play. But before Logan could field the ball, Hoak stepped in front while running to third. He fielded the ball barehanded, flipped the ball to the confused Logan and trotted off the field. The umpires ruled Hoak out for being "hit" with a batted ball but Post received credit for a single and Bell advanced to second. That play caused a minor sensation. Arthur Daley in the New York Times quoted the 'baseball men' (a group whose identity is seemingly more secret than the Illuminati) as wondering if 'Master Donald' had opened a Pandora's Box, ushering in a new era of players interfering with balls in play. Of course, it was nothing of the sort as National League President Warren Giles (working with American League Umpire-in-Chief, Cal Hubbard) soon modified the rule so that any time that a runner intentionally interfered with a ball in play resulted in both the runner and the batter called out, and no advancement by any other runners.

As a youngster, Hoak tried professional boxing but after seven straight losses and a few good beatings, he tried his hand at baseball. He broke into the Major Leagues in 1954 after a stint in the United States Marines and one season in Cuba. Word has it that during his one season in Cuba, Hoak actually batted against Fidel Castro, who was a law student at the time. According to The Second Fireside Book of Baseball, Castro and some friends commandeered the park where Hoak's team was playing. Castro took some warm-up pitches, turned to face Hoak in the batter's box, called out the Spanish equivalent of "Batter up!" and pitched. He was wild, and threw several pitches near Hoak's head. After a few "dusters," Hoak turned to the umpire and said, "Get that idiot out of the game!" The umpire obliged, and spoke to some park policemen, who marched Castro off the field. During his two seasons with the Dodgers, Hoak shared third base duties with Jackie Robinson and Billy Cox. In 1955, his Dodgers defeated the New York Yankees in the World Series to win their only championship in Brooklyn. Dem Bums finally did it, and Hoak earned a World Series ring in his sophomore year of Major League Baseball. Hoak played third base in place of Robinson in the seventh and deciding game of that Series - the only World Series game Robinson did not play in during his career.

In 1969, the year that my beloved Mets won the World Series, Don Hoak passed away. He served in the marines in World War II and had a tremendous baseball history, including two World Series victories. He is memorialized in the famous photograph with Johnny Podres and Roy Campanella, celebrating their 1955 World Series win against the New York Yankees.

(*"Dem Bums" moment of glory*)

Unfortunately, the Dodgers unloaded Hoak in a five player deal with the Chicago Cubs, which landed him in the Windy City. The Dodgers felt that Hoak was not a capable enough third baseman, and wanted Randy 'Handsome Ransom' Jackson as the replacement for Jackie Robinson. Hoak was a Cub for only one season before moving on to the Cincinnati Reds in another five player deal. In Cincinnati, Hoak hooked up with Manager George "Birdie" Tebbetts, who took a keen interest in Hoak. In a 1961 interview, Hoak told Sports Illustrated writer, Walter Bingham, "Tebbetts taught me everything." Birdie changed Hoak's batting stance, and built up his confidence, telling him that he was a better player than he thought he was. Hoak hit.293 for Tebbetts and drove in 89 runs. In that same interview, Hoak repeated one of Tebbetts' favorite expressions:

"I can't understand a player who won't give you 90 feet."

Coincidentally, Harvey Haddix and Don Hoak were both members of the Red Legs, and were traded together to the Pirates in 1959, for a guy named Charles "Whammy" Douglas, and few other players. Whammy didn't make the team after the trade, and never played again.

Hoak had toiled in the Pirates' farm system and managed at each level. His dream was to be the Pittsburgh Pirates Manager. Seven games into the 1969 season, Larry Shepard was fired after finishing fourth in the American League East. The understanding between Hoak and the Pirates owners was that the job was his. Instead, the Pirates rehired Danny Murtaugh; Hoak was devastated. Later that day, he saw two thieves stealing his brother-in-law's car. He chased them for a few blocks, suffered a heart attack and collapsed in the street, passing away a few hours later. Don Hoak was 41.

The next most important person in the "Harvey Haddix" game is Joe Adcock. Joe and Harvey go way back to 1954 when Adcock ricocheted a ball off of Harvey's knee. Arthroscopic surgery hadn't been invented back then so Harvey suffered knee pain from that day forward. Similar to Mickey Mantle's debilitating knee injury, Harvey soldiered on to play in three All Star games and to win a World Series. Five years after his knee was shattered by Joe Adcock's mighty bat, lightning struck again as Joe homered in the historic thirteenth inning, with the hit that handed Harvey a loss during the greatest game ever pitched. Simply put, Joe was bad luck for Harvey. Many years later, after Harvey's death, Adcock was interviewed about that game. Adcock said, "He knew what he had in mind when he let the ball loose. The wind had been blowing in all night and maybe it was a freak because when I came to bat, the flag in center field was still. I was thinking he'd been keeping the ball away from me all night and maybe he'd do it again and he did and I hit it." Adcock is as well-known for that game as Harvey. The guy that ruins perfection in baseball seems to always be as well-known as the person searching for it.

EVERYBODY IN THE POOL

Of all my friends, we were the only ones who had an in-ground pool, or any pool for that matter. My father was exorbitantly cheap and every home purchase was treated just like the epic showdown with the redwood furniture Indians. So, how did we wind up having a swimming pool? The answer to that question goes back to the Bronx on East Tremont Avenue, at my grandparent's house. They had a two story brownstone on Tremont Avenue that had five bedrooms, four of which were inhabited by aging war-torn soldiers. One room even had a real hospital bed, and an IV stand. From time to time when one of the soldiers would pass away, she would be the recipient of their money. It was often a few thousand dollars, or more. My grandmother was generous and would slip money to my mother without my father knowing. One time, it was a lot of money and my mother was nervous that my father would find out. So my grandmother gave the money to my father, but made him sign an agreement stating that he would only use the money to have a pool installed for all of us to enjoy. If he used the money in some other way, she would send Mr. Ferris (her personal lawyer) after him and he would never see another dollar from her ever again. She also said she would call his job and let them know that he beat his wife and children and have him fired.

I learned how to vacuum the pool, measure and administer the chemicals, empty the debris (including bugs and toads) from the skimmers and of course, remove the leaves! One day when we were roughhousing in the pool, my father said "Be careful, some poor guy died for this pool!" He told us that my grandmother would smother the men with a pillow, and clean out their savings accounts. There's nothing like the comforting words of a father! He told us it was a good thing that we used my grandmother's money for the pool; otherwise, it would have disappeared at the racetrack on a horse headed for the glue factory. Was this actually true? Who knows? Almost every day he told our beagle, Princess, that she was headed for the glue factory.

(Who really paid for this pool?)

111

I knew my grandmother loved the racetrack. She spent almost every Friday night in Yonkers, where she won and lost fortunes. I sure hoped those veterans I met in her home weren't smothered with pillows. Then I thought about the bleach and realized that I was scared of her a little bit. Did she smother anyone with a pillow? Why didn't she smother my father with a pillow? That was the real question. Grandma was so, so nice to me. When I think about those veterans, I have to wonder if they survived a world war, just to die under one of my grandmother's pillows.

> **I guess it's a bit like Don Hoak. He survived World War II,
> a boxing and baseball career, but dies chasing the guy
> who stole his brother-in-law's car. It wasn't even his car.**

I recently called Harvey's widow to give her an update on the progress of the book. I want her to know that I'm learning a lot about Harvey, as well as a lot about myself. If feel that I'm seeking out her permission – or perhaps her approval. Just like our last call, she is cheerful and wonderful. I offer to send my manuscript for her to review. I tell her proudly of my interview with Hank and we talk about the smoking thing. She tells me that the cigarette company always made sure that Harvey got his cigarettes during the off season, as well. I tell her that every person I have spoken with mentions what a great person Harvey was, as well as a beloved pitching coach. We discuss the recent re-broadcast of the 1960 World Series and I could tell that she was extremely pleased. She was even sent a DVD of the game by Major League Baseball.

THE DOG MONEY

When I was away at college, I received a call from my mom. My younger brother, Todd, was attacked by a German Shepherd. Fighting off the dog, Todd suffered a series of lacerations and needed stitches and medical care. He had inherited my old paper route, which brought him down Blydenburgh Road. I remember that dog well. Occasionally he would break his leash and chase me as I pedaled for dear life. Thankfully, he only got close enough to nip me once or twice. It was much worse for Todd. What my mother didn't tell me was that when my brother returned home bleeding from his face and other parts of his body, the very first thing my father did was race off to Woolworth's to purchase a Polaroid camera and film. That Woolworth's was at the end of Blydenburgh Road, the same path my brother took before the attack. Rather than taking my brother to a hospital, he propped my brother up on the front porch to pose for a pictorial of his wounds. Only after the film was used up and the evidence was properly documented did he take Todd to the hospital.

As my brother tells it, my father smelled money right away. He became a modern day Kojak – he found the house and the dog, brought a local detective to their house, and even called my grandmother for her legal counsel. About a year later, a check for $25,000 arrived, although we never really learned the exact amount. From then on it was always referred to as 'the dog money.' That was a lot of money in 1979 and many would say that it's quite a bit now. My father told my brother that the dog money was going toward his college, and he would receive it on the day that he left to further his education.

So every year as my brother got closer to college, he would inquire about 'the dog money'. He actually finished high school a year early, to escape living with The Hand. My brother is much smarter than me. Why the hell didn't I think of that? As Todd and I were preparing for his first year, and my return to college, Todd wanted to firm up that 'the dog money' is intact. My father went absolutely berserk

(*The German Shepherd Survivor*)

114

and within a matter of seconds, they were nearly in a fistfight. My father yelled that he knew this day would come, and the money went towards our breakfast, lunch and dinner, chlorine for the pool and the roof over our heads. Neither of us mentioned that a few months after the check arrived, my dad traded in his junky 18 ft. mosquito boat for a new, 27 ft. Bayliner. We drove off, both of us thinking of the lesson we just learned. Money brings evil. My father gained a bigger boat, but lost both of his sons. He actually lost me long before that, but that was definitely the day he lost Todd.

MRS. HADDIX

It's been about three years since I worked up the courage to call Marcia Haddix for the first time. Now I finally have a manuscript for my book and wanted to talk with her again. I think at first she was shocked I was still writing it, and equally shocked that I actually finished. I let Mrs. Haddix know the manuscript was on its way to her, and she could add whatever she liked. I wanted it to be authentic, and do Harvey justice. Waiting for her response was just like waiting to see if I made the eighth great basketball team again. Her opinion was hugely important to me. If she hated it, where do I go from here? So I agonized, and waited, and tossed and turned, and then the package came to me in the mail. Her thoughts and edits are below.

January 25, 2014

Dear Stephen:

When your manuscript arrived, my first thought was how long it would take to read all that. After reading the first few pages, I couldn't put it down and finished it on the spot.

Harv would have been flattered to know you admired him and considered him a hero. When MLB took his "perfect game" from him; it was a crushing blow. As I ranted about it, Harv said "I know what I did." His perfect game was swept under the rug after that. In 2009, when real baseball fans recalled the 50th anniversary of Harv's game, the Pirates chose to ignore it. Had Harv been here, that would have been another blow. The Pirates may have been embarrassed since their carelessness had allowed everything in the Three Rivers Stadium Museum to be stolen. Harv had loaned his uniform from his perfect game to the museum. When Cooperstown asked for the uniform, we found out it was gone. When I was in Pittsburgh in 2010, the surviving 1960 Pirates and Mrs. Clemente were honored before the game. I sat in the stands wondering who won two of those games in the World Series? That was more than a little insulting.

As I read your story, I made notes to call to your attention. None are important so you may or may not change anything. *(Editor's note – Mrs. Haddix's corrections have been incorporated where possible, with our gratitude.)*

Chapter 2:

Harv's family lived on a farm 30 miles north of Medway. The family midwife lived in Medway. Harv's Mother went there only to have babies. After ten days, she went back to the farm. Harv was always sorry he mentioned Medway on his stats.

I understood there were over 380 young men in Columbus for the tryouts. Harv didn't get to throw the first day and went back the second day. Only three were signed and Harv was the only one who made it to the Majors. Also, Brecheen is pronounced Brick-Keen.

Chapter 9:

Lew died from lung cancer and Harv died from emphysema.

Chapter 14:

Harv's first year in the minors was in Winston-Salem, home of R. J. Reynolds. He was 22 and never smoked. In spite of it, Harv loved Winston-Salem and still holds the strike out record in the Carolina League.

Chapter 24:

Don Hoak was a character. He claimed to be an ex-marine. Someone in Pittsburgh investigated and said Don was in the Navy Band. Who knows?

We have a picture of Harv being carried off the field after Adcock's line drive to his knee. Harv picked up the ball, threw Adcock out, and passed out. His knee-cap was separated. Musial was quoted as saying Harv could never pitch as good after that. That is a matter of opinion.

All in all, I loved your book. You don't have to change a thing. Loved your description of your relatives. Harv had relatives comparable. He and his brothers had nicknames for them - none flattering. I always told Harv he and his three brothers were raised like a pack of wolves. His parents were uneducated and had little else but a work ethic to teach them. Harv worked hard to accomplish what he did. He said he wished he was 6'5" and weighed 200 lbs. so he wouldn't have to work so hard.

Harv would have loved your opinion on eating crabs. He couldn't believe the people of Baltimore and their love of crabs. He said crabs are scavengers and "I don't eat scavengers."

Thank you for letting me read your book. It was a treat to read facts about Harv instead of figments of someone's imagination. Our family is anxiously waiting to read your book. Good luck and keep writing.

Best Wishes,

Marcia Haddix

Marcia Haddix

Harvey, I was introduced to baseball as a little leaguer. Like you, I was a left-handed pitcher. I was tall and thin but I could throw pretty hard and had a curve ball before the other kids. My favorite days were game days, especially if I was pitching. I remember getting to the field early and trying to peek at the coach's scorecard to see if I was pitching. Even at nine years old, seeing your name written on the scorecard is a big thrill. Off I go!

In preparation for the day I could leave home, I got a job as soon as I could. I worked three jobs to save up for a car and still, the only one I could get barely ran. That was the first in a long line of clunkers. The good news is that as much as I hated that car, all of that was replaced with the joy I felt when I was able to give my daughter a little black Mercedes for her 17th birthday. Witnessing her happiness that day was worth driving clunkers my entire life.

It was a scorching hot August day in 1979, and my seemingly eternal countdown away from The Hand has finally come to an end. My second or third clunker, a lime green 1973 Vega complete with a new engine from my grandmother, (that I hope that nobody had to die for it) was headed west for Indiana State University. I packed my baseball mitt, cleats, three drawers of clothes, my Farrah Fawcett and Julius Erving posters, and my hopes and dreams into that car - the embodiment of what I saw as my ticket to the rest of my life, or rather, the best of my life. As I was cruising toward my destiny, I put what was left of my Bronx accent away in the glove box, forever. It was time to live. My life had just begun.

Every sundrenched mile was my own; it was the ride of my life. Every mile further from home and closer to campus increased my sense of security. Knowing that the distance between me and father was growing, was cathartic. This colossal albatross had been lifted and everyday would be what I wanted to do, when I wanted to do it. Harvey, I know the feeling of perfection. I thought about my first pitch, my first newspaper article, my first apartment.

College! It was a word that rang my bell of freedom.

POKE THE BEAR

You have reached the end of the book, but I needed to add a 'Poke the Bear' chapter. As my good friend, Laura Waage, is fond of telling me,

Yes, I love to poke the bear.

Laura is a nationally-renowned, brilliant social networking person. She is super-smart about everything. We have had numerous deep conversations about what is important in life and what is the meaning of success. When I think about success I think of all the fun I have had in life - the laughter, the great times, the forging of new friendships, lending a hand, putting a smile on someone's face, giving advice that worked out well…and of course, finding true friendship in a few of my childhood heroes. That's just icing on the cake for me. I am happy, and I am blessed.

My successes have nothing to do with something I bought, or the amount of my bank balance. For a long time, I had no money and no accounts. It's not a very good feeling. Laura has told me that I was smart, confident and savvy enough to be a billionaire. I asked her why I wasn't a billionaire. Her answer was because I like to poke the bear. I mess with the people I love, I do what I love, I chase what I believe and I have a good time every step of the way. I've seldom chased after money. I'm not a billionaire, but you can only water ski behind one boat. If I tell you I'm doing something, I'm doing it with 100% of my effort. If I say I'll be there, I'll be there. My billion is the happiness and well-being of my family and friends. This is my good fortune and this is my happily ever after.

EPILOGUE

"**I**'ll have the shrimp marinara, no pasta and a Corona," was the way our relationship started. That was Stephen's order at the world famous Vincent's Clam Bar the first time we met. I am Harlan Friedman, owner of the Harlan Agency, a PR, Marketing and Event consulting company, whose life would forever change on that faithful day. Over the past several years Stephen has been a client, a mentor, a best friend and at times even a philosophy teacher to me. Albeit humble about his own accomplishments and connectivity, by simply knowing him you are immediately a better person. Through our relationship I have improved my business, accomplished some of my childhood dreams and truly feel that I have become a stronger personality.

Currently, Stephen Costello is the Executive Vice President of Steiner Sports Marketing, a division of Omnicom Group, a leading global advertising and marketing communications services company. Steiner Sports marketing is the leading producer of authentic hand-signed collectibles and the best source for all your sports gift and collectible needs. Steiner Sports marketing also plans and executes more than 500 events each year ranging from speaking engagements and fantasy clinics to product endorsements and athlete meet & greets. Stephen is most proud of the company's charity division, which partners annually with over 300 non-profit organizations to provide unique and authentic sports memorabilia, one-of-a-kind sports experiences, and customized products for charity auctions and events. Stephen's work in the field and reputation amongst athletes, clients and customers alike has made him a frequent guest of the WFAN and CBS TV smash morning show, "The Boomer and Carton Show," on Fox and Friends, YES Network's "Memories of the Game," Fox Business and CNN.

Stephen also works as a mentor and business advisor to many. He has taken the internship program of Steiner Sports under his wing and helps prep these young people for the real world. Stephen also has become a regular lecturer at Universities and companies throughout the Northeast. His business approach, social media strategies and sense of focusing on your goals and achieving them are some of the captivating topics that keep his audiences engaged. These topics, mixed with relevant stories of the athletes he works with on a daily basis, may make a very interesting follow-up to this book.

Through all of his professional accomplishments it is his personal ones that put the biggest smile on his face. To unwind, Stephen now regularly enjoys 40-mile bike rides throughout the Hamptons and spending time on the basketball and tennis courts. In Stephen's own words, the 'most amazing thing to complete his life' is his family. Wife Elaine, daughters Samantha and Madison and puppies Buddy and Kuno are truly the core of who Stephen is and why he does what he does. Growing up in a chaotic home, Stephen has built a beautiful, relaxing and nurturing environment for his loved ones to dwell. Outside of the home, the koi pond, tennis court and wooded acreage give the appearance of a life well lived. The inside of the home is filled with love, encouragement and great vibes.

I've stood with Stephen at so many unbelievable moments. Talking with baseball greats such as Derek Jeter, Mariano Rivera and Don Larsen, to hearing Stanley Cup tales from the NY Rangers locker room, from Mark Messier himself, Stephen's professional life would be interpreted as epic by most. As our relationship grows and his life as an author continues, I look forward to standing witness and hearing so many more of these stories.

-Harlan Friedman

(Steve and his family)

AFTERWORD

By Samantha Costello

Throughout my childhood, I heard many stories about my dad growing up in the Bronx. Those stories and my experiences with my dad have made me realize how great of a dad I have. He is family-first and would do anything for my sister and me. While his father never took him to a baseball game, he and I went to more games than I could count. However, there are five games I will never forget.

(Me at my first World Series game)

In 2000, New York saw its first subway series between the Yankees and the Mets. It was the first time the Mets were in the World Series since 1986 and the first time the Mets and Yankees played each other in the World Series. The Yankees were the defending champions and would win again, by beating my Mets in five games. I was nine years old. My mom didn't want me going because she thought I would miss school the day after the games, but my dad and I went to every game in that series. We got home most nights between one and two o'clock in the morning and I made sure that I got to school on time.

Because my dad works in the industry, I must say that going to a game with my dad was probably a bit different other kids going with their dads. And unlike my dad, I was fortunate enough to get everything from foam fingers to autograph baseballs, to more. Before the first World Series game, my dad took me out for an early dinner. When we got there, I found out dinner was with the Mets manager Bobby Valentine. There were about a dozen police officers near our table making sure nobody got near us. After dinner I not only got a picture with the Mets manager but I got a picture with all the police officers. At nine years old that was probably the first time I thought about law enforcement, and now am currently pursuing a career in that field.

(Me and some of New York City's finest)

The series ended at five games. I was sad because the Mets lost, but also because my dad and I weren't going to anymore World Series games that year. The Mets only won one game in that series (game three) but with that game, they broke the Yankees' fourteen game World Series winning streak. My favorite player was Mike Piazza; throughout my childhood, I always wore #31 no matter what sport I was playing. I loved watching Mike Piazza play and because he was a good friend of my dad's, I even got to meet him as well as many other Mets players from that team. Of the four home runs hit in the 2000 World Series, Mike Piazza hit three of them.

For years I heard about this book my dad would someday write. I'm surprised it's finally here. Reading the book gave me the opportunity to learn even more about my dad. I've heard some of these stories throughout the years, but the ones that were new to me really had me laughing. All kids want to go to a baseball game, whether they're baseball fans or not. It's a memory that will always stay in your mind, and you will always remember the great moments within that game. This book is all about memories. My father has many of them from his family and our family. Some of his memories are good, and others are horrible, but we can look back on them with a smile.

My dad made a point to never be like his dad. He provided for us, and did anything and everything he could for us. Dad did it without ever holding anything over our heads. He loved to tell us his "growing up" stories and how

(My father and I)

hard things were for him. Knowing my grandfather like I do, man do I believe things were hard for my dad! If I can say one thing, it's that dad and I went to a bunch of games and I loved them all.

-Sam Costello

Mom, your son is now an author. Start calling people up!

Elaine, God bless the broken road that brought me straight to you. You're truly amazing and possibly not human. You complete me.

Sam and **Madison**, you have given me more joy than I thought I could have in my life. You are both my everything. Sam, never stop breaking balls and shackling people. Madison, nothing beats watching you sing and perform. You make me proud crazy every day.

Todd, how much would the dog money be today? You surpass the meaning of brother in every way.

Craig, good things lie ahead.

Brandon and **Mara**, thanks for having me in your family and your company, I am humbled by your work on and off the field.

Gitomer, you're the Tommy Agee of my literary world.

Doug, thanks for your friendship and words.

Harvey, you pitched a helluva game.

Pop, you were the kindest man I ever knew, I miss you every day.

Gregg and **Pam**, you are two extraordinary friends in every way, thank you for over twenty five years of love, laughter and lifelong memories.

Weathy, proud to call you my friend and a true Giant in every way.

Grandma, I miss the B-12 shots and the cube steaks,
and I don't think we ever got the ship back.

Stevie Cohen, my brother and uncle to my kids.
You have always been there for us!

Bobby and **Gina** it's hard to find words for how special you are,
and what you mean to us...even in a book.

Neuman, you taught me the power of follow-up correspondence, and
that was a game changer for me. You were never trying to teach me
but I was always learning from you. Team resources was an amazing
concept way ahead of it's time. You might beat me one on one, but I
will always have a better outside shot.

Mahoney, the most loyal guy in the world,
you make everyday fun for me.

Zak, I'm brilliant because you're always
three feet away with the answer.

MY BOOK TEAM

Here's a special thank you from the bottom of my heart for putting the wind in my sails, giving me your wisdom, and believing in me.

Tara, what can I say, you're the funny Italian sister I never had, and a part time editor, and full time cheerleader.

Madison, thanks for editing, and bringing your beautiful voice and spirit to our editing sessions. Thanks for reminding me that was then, and this is now.

Harlen, thanks for taking the ride with me.

Carli, glad to make this the start of your PR career.

Zak, a voice of reason, and a co-pilot, I wont forget walking by you on the plane to see you editing!

Lauren, the first of our many projects, glad you were brought into my book and life.

Peter Shankman, I didn't deserve the help you gave me.

Sam, your afterward was why I wake up everyday.

Gitomer, I didn't deserve your help either.

Jessica, thanks for everything, my next book may have a chapter on letting book team members borrow your car! Maybe two chapters!

Kate, I guess the Yankees taught you to hit them where they ain't. So many ideas I would have never thought of!

Chris, you were glue and my creative genius, you brought the story to life. You are told as a kid you can't judge a book by it's cover. You can judge this book by it's cover I assure you. This book was designed by Chris Messina (MadeByMessina.com) and he brought to the book strong winds for the sails, and helped bring my life to life through imagery I could never have imagined with my own two eyes. Our journey went from my grade school street corner in the Bronx to shoot photos, to my dining room table in Westhampton to make edits, plus a few hundred phone calls in between. I'm sure this will not be the only book for either of us but it will always be the first book.

Thank you Chris, you are a game changer.

Made in the USA
Charleston, SC
06 December 2014